Fabricating Identities

# Working with Culture on the Edge
## Edited by Vaia Touna, University of Alabama

This series of small books draws on revised versions of posts that originally appeared online at edge.ua.edu – the blog for Culture on the Edge, a research collaborative engaged in rethinking identity studies. Each chapter is complemented by an original response from an early career scholar outside the group, that presses the chapter in new directions, either by applying its approach to novel situations or by offering a critique that enhances the approach. Each volume in the series therefore demonstrates how to work with a more dynamic, historically-sensitive approach to identity, as exemplified at a host of ordinary social sites – on varied themes, from museums and popular music to ordering at fast-food restaurants. The brief chapters retain the informality of blogging, modeling for readers how scholars can better examine the contingent and therefore changeable practices that help to create the conditions in which we claim to be an enduring something.

Each volume opens with a brief general Introduction to the key word on which it focuses and ends with an Afterword that tackles wider issues of relevance to the volume's main theme.

Ideal for a variety of classes in which identity or the past are discussed, these small books can either set the table for more in-depth readings in a course or be paired with their suggested resources to comprise an entire course's readings. Thoroughly collaborative, cross-disciplinary, and cross-generational in nature, *Working with Culture on the Edge* provides an opportunity to rethink identity with a group of scholars committed to pressing identity studies in new directions.

Published:

*Fabricating Difference*
Edited by Steven W. Ramey

*Fabricating Origins*
Edited by Russell T. McCutcheon

# Fabricating Identities

Edited by
Russell T. McCutcheon

eQuinox

SHEFFIELD UK   BRISTOL CT

Published by Equinox Publishing Ltd.

UK:     Office 415, The Workstation, 15 Paternoster Row, Sheffield, South Yorkshire S1 2BX

USA:     ISD, 70 Enterprise Drive, Bristol, CT 06010

www.equinoxpub.com

First published 2017

British Library Cataloguing-in-Publication Data
A catalogue record for this book is available from the British Library.

ISBN-13  978 1 78179 496 8  (hardback)
ISBN-13  978 1 78179 497 5  (paperback)

Library of Congress Cataloging-in-Publication Data
Names: McCutcheon, Russell T., 1961- author.
Title: Fabricating identities / edited by Russell T. McCutcheon.
Description: Sheffield, UK ; Bristol, CT : Equinox Publishing, Ltd., [2017] |
Series: Working with culture on the edge ; volume 3 | Includes index. |
Identifiers: LCCN 2016055123 (print) | LCCN 2017036662 (ebook) |
ISBN 9781781795880 (ePDF) | ISBN 9781781794968 (hb) |
ISBN 9781781794975 (pb)
Subjects: LCSH: Identity (Psychology) | Characters and characteristics.
Classification: LCC BF697 (ebook) | LCC BF697 .F24 2017 (print) |
DDC 155.2--dc23
LC record available at https://lccn.loc.gov/2016055123

Typeset by S.J.I. Services, New Delhi
Printed and bound by Lightning Source Inc. (La Vergne, TN), Lightning Source UK Ltd. (Milton Keynes), Lightning Source AU Pty. (Scoresby, Victoria).

# Contents

*Preface*                                                                viii

Introduction                                                                1
   *Russell T. McCutcheon*

1.  Who Are You? I'm a Religious Studies Scholar            10
       *K. Merinda Simmons*

2.  Am I a Religious Studies Scholar?                           13
       *David G. Robertson*

3.  Who Are You? I'm Wednesday's Child                       20
       *Craig Martin*

4.  Seeing the Forest *and* the Trees                            23
       *Sarah Levine*

5.  Who Are You? I'm Greek                                        29
       *Vaia Touna*

6.  You're Greek? Well…, I'm (Northern) Irish, Kinda…     34
       *Christopher R. Cotter*

7.  Who Are You? I'm a Miser                                     42
       *Steven W. Ramey*

8.  Contesting Labels and the Study of Religion            45
       *Anja Kirsch*

9.  Who Are You? I'm a Leg Crosser                             51
       *Russell T. McCutcheon*

10. Who Am I? Merely a Player                                   55
       *Candace Mixon*

11. Who Are You? I'm a Feminist                               61
    *Leslie Dorrough Smith*

12. Atheism and Its Consequences                            66
    *Ian Alexander Cuthbertson*

13. Who Are You? I'm a Vegetarian                           73
    *Steven W. Ramey*

14. You Are What You Eat                                    76
    *Sarah E. Dees*

15. Who Are You? I'm an Alabamian                           82
    *Russell T. McCutcheon*

16. Secrecy, Stories, and Boundaries                        89
    *Emily A. Schmidt*

17. Who Are You? I'm Vaia and I'm Touna                     95
    *Vaia Touna*

18. "Naaaaaw, You Show Me YOUR ID"                          99
    *Richard Newton*

19. Who Are You? I'm a New Mom                             105
    *K. Merinda Simmons*

20. I'm a Soon-to-be Dad                                   110
    *Jason W.M. Ellsworth*

21. Who Are You? I Am/Am Not a McCutcheonite               116
    *Craig Martin*

22. I Know You Are, But What Am I?                         119
    *Stacie Swain*

23. Who Are You? I'm Short (...and Cute)      128
     *Leslie Dorrough Smith*

24. I'm "Irish," Torontonian, ...French?      132
     *Matthew Sheedy*

     Afterword: Express Yourself      139
     *Russell T. McCutcheon*

     *Index*      165

# Preface

The series in which this volume appears is intended as a collection of pithy but nonetheless intellectually weighty introductions to topics that, in the estimation of our group, deserve rethinking. That we are all scholars of religion who do not feel compelled to see ourselves simply talking about whatever it is that people define as religion is itself part of that rethinking – but in this series we tackle topics that, hopefully, will be of far wider interest, such as this volume's focus on identity. Moreover, despite being succinct volumes with short, easily read chapters (making them ideal, we think, for use in undergraduate classes), the series does more work than at first appears, since all of the respondents, or better put commentators, are people at far earlier stages of their career than those to whom they reply. The chapters are arranged in pairs since the second author was invited to use the work of the first (which began life as a blog post) as a springboard into issues of relevance to the volume's effort to make the commonsense understanding of identity (i.e., as an essential, internal trait) our object of study; and, as editor, I eagerly awaited those chapters to be submitted so that I could see where each respondent landed. I'm happy to report that I was not disappointed – which, I think, means that scholars currently working on their PhD degrees, or those fresh from having completed and defended their dissertations, have much to say about where our intellectual pursuits ought to be going. My hope is that this volume is one among the many places where their claims can be heard and considered.

My thanks to Vaia Touna, my colleague at the University of Alabama and the editor of this book series, for her interest in the topic of this volume, and also to Janet Joyce, of Equinox Publishers, for her longtime and enthusiastic commitment to publishing work in the study of religion that presses a few of the usually unspoken boundaries of the field. And finally, my thanks to Andie Alexander for producing the index for the volume.

# Introduction

## Russell T. McCutcheon

...there is no such thing as identity, only operational acts of identification. The identities we talk about so pompously, as if they existed independently of those who express them, are made (and unmade) only through the mediation of such identificatory acts, in short, by their enunciation. (Bayart 2005: 92)

Culture on the Edge is a scholarly working group, begun in the Spring of 2012 and comprised of scholars of religion working in North America, whose aim is to use social theory to offer more nuanced understandings of how those things that we commonly call identities are produced, managed, and continually reproduced in competitive social economies. We are, to rephrase it, scholars of religion who happen to think that our tools are applicable far more widely than just the study of religion; this is not because, as some (inside our field and well outside of it, too) might argue, religion is the mystical basis to all that is significant but, instead, because we all agree that both religion and the very act of calling something religious are utterly mundane aspects of our modern world – so mundane that an adequate understanding of religion presupposes an adequate understanding of how any act of designation and signification takes place. Culture on the Edge, then, was born of a frustration with how just some acts are often set apart by scholars and we are forbidden to inquire into them any further (to nod toward Emile Durkheim's still relevant definition of religion), as if they were inexplicably significant all along – rather than seeing that very *act* of setting apart, of naming and distinguishing, of drawing lines and policing boundaries, as the way that significance was brought into being in the first place.

Given the current wealth of studies on identity that presume it to be an inner trait somehow projected out into the world – a common enough folk model in our society, whereby we all seem to assume some intangible, inner somethingness is "expressed" from the inside out – it seemed to us reasonable to apply our skills in this one (admittedly broad) domain; after all, the presumption of religious experience being the pristine inner ground for outer action and organization has a long history in our field, one against which we work as scholars of religion who are interested in the social and the historical. Why not tackle the analogous set of problems associated with assuming that identity is merely a secondary expression of some mysterious and ethereal inner force?

The ease with which identity is presumed to be an inner trait only later projected into the public domain is pretty easy to document; and since this seems to be our default way of talking about it, it makes thinking anew about how identity works rather difficult – for how to entertain that our "talking about it" might precede it, might be the very way in which a sense of an "it" is made in the first place? For example, consider the popular animated 2015 film, *Inside Out* as but one easy illustration of this widespread folk model: motive forces deep inside us, associated there with certain emotional states, drive our actions (the proverbial "ghost in the machine" model, in fact). Identity then ends up being an internal quality only subsequently expressed for others to see, making social interaction the effect of prior and private sentiments. The film's popularity – due to a host of factors, no doubt – is thus at least partly based on how it reproduces and thereby confirms this familiar (and perhaps comforting?) model for its viewers.[1]

But despite this being the commonsense understanding that we all probably have of ourselves, Culture on the Edge has consistently tried to press an alternative model, one that argues for the self as being a social and thus situational and historical product through and through. It's counter-intuitive, to be sure, but there are plenty

---

[1]  The example I'm about to describe derives from a June 24, 2015, blog post entitled "Look How Tall You Are."

of mundane sites where you can experiment with reconceptualizing identity in this alternative way. The chapters in this book provide quite an array, but I thought I'd offer one here, to start with – to prime the pump, as it were. (The Afterword provides a few more examples – all of which are things that are good to think with, at least when trying to rethink identity.)

I bet lots of us had our heights measured and marked, from time to time, against a wall or doorpost as we were growing up. I certainly remember my parents doing this. What's useful about this example is how nicely we can see the way a subject's identity is formed by the application (which is itself an act we can watch happening), by others, of a grid or classification (or, we could also say, value) system. In my case, it was a yardstick – the metric system hadn't yet hit Canada's shores.

It's an instance of what the French social theorist, Louis Althusser, termed *interpellation* – the process by which one's subjectivity is formed in a collaborative public setting, in which one is addressed or treated in this or that way and which then leads to one taking on this or that identity, and thus place, within a diverse (and usually hierarchical) system. While his well-known example was being hailed by a police officer, and in that moment taking on the subjectivity of "suspect," we could just as easily consider the more routine example of how the unexpected knock on the apartment door one Saturday morning suddenly prompts you to "see" your apartment *as* messy or yourself *as* underdressed and therefore in no position to entertain guests. In the seconds prior to the knock neither of these concerns was an issue to you; but the chagrin or embarrassment or worry (or whatever it is you feel once you hear the knock, once you know that unannounced guests have arrived) is the internalized residue of a prior social situation.

Thinking back to height, children are probably not naturally rushing to measure how tall they are, for they likely don't even know that they're growing and changing – it's so gradual, who can see it happening to themselves? But mom and dad know changes are coming, and they're the ones who are keen to know if their child is ahead or behind the curve. (How early did they talk? When did they take their first steps? What grade did they get in math? Making evident that distinction does not just distinguish but ranks.) So the application, by others, of a grid not of our choosing (does the young child even know what an inch is, much less a decimeter?), results in a little pencil line and a date written on the doorframe (not insignificantly in someone else's handwriting, by the way), against which we quite literally learn to measure ourselves at some future point in time. And sooner or later we find enough marks there that we can start telling a developmental narrative about ourselves, about then versus now, which anticipates a future (that's not yet even happened): "When will I be taller?" or "When will you be fully grown?"

And it's that narrative, given to us by others (not unlike that surprising knock on the door), created by means of devices not of our making, that unseats the taken-for-granted and uninterrupted existence of the young child, in which life occupies the eternal present; it's an existence shattered no less by persistent "What are you going to be when you grow up?" questions that many adults seem driven to (im)pose – questions that unsettle the innocence of the youthful present by judging it in comparison to an imagined future for which the question-asker cares far more than the question-recipient.

So that little child who stands up straight against the wall (the one who now "feels proud" concerning how "tall" they are ["Look at you: you're a big girl!"], or "short" and so a little dejected) is a good example of the social fabrication of the self, of a specific site of identification, of the manner in which others create the subjects we then learn to take ourselves to be, by placing a grid on us and plotting us in relation to their concerns – people who are themselves being measured in countless ways and asked questions of their own by yet others who have concerns of their own ("What will you do with that degree?" "How much do you make?" or "When will you retire?").

And so on, and so on. All the way down.

The members of Culture on the Edge tackle this very rethinking, at a variety of social sites, examining the contradiction between, on the one hand, the historicity of identity (which is now generally seen by scholars to be always fluid over place and time and continually performed), and, on the other, the nagging presumption we all seem to have of a static and ahistorical (call it primordial) origin (like that pencil line on the wall or doorframe) against which historical and cultural change is thought to be measured. For if scholars today rightly critique notions of speaking "proper English" (inasmuch as such a position normalizes but one mode of speech – that of economic and political elites – among countless variants) then they should probably also address the problem of presuming that cultural change is premised on the distinction between a primordial and static origin, on the one hand, and its subsequent derivations (i.e., the premise of much contemporary diaspora, hybridity, and creolization studies in which we examine the change at the margin as compared to the center/origin) on the other. The problem, at least for the social theorist, of course, is that the center is itself just as fluid as that margin – and, what's more, it is only the center for a certain group, with certain interests; change the interests and innumerable other spots on the map will become yet new centers with edges all their own. Employing the example of the once (and still) widely used scholarly notion of syncretism, we can make the point as follows: if "culture" is a word that scholars use to name elements of the complex, historical web of diverse human practices that, at a given moment, catch someone's attention (so as to generalize about something, say, in the world called "Italian culture"), then what more have we said about a particular set of historically determined human practices when we label it syncretistic? For the supposed sources from which the hybrid blend derives are themselves *always and already* complexly blended and thus no less ambiguous or derivative. The problem, then, is how to examine change in identity over time and place without normalizing, by dehistoricizing, but one among any historical, human practice's countless beginnings?

Following such examples as the work of Jean-François Bayart (currently the chairman of the Fonds d'analyse des sociétés politiques and a senior research fellow at the Centre national de la recherche scientifique [CNRS]), in particular his 1996 book, *The Illusion of Cultural Identity* (English translation: 2005), we propose moving from studying identity, or presupposing it to be either stable or the projection of an inner sentiment that is somehow externalized in the public domain, and, instead, recognizing that scholars study discrete strategies of identification and the situationally-specific techniques for fabricating the impression of authenticity, autonomy, and primordiality – operations that, despite how they may at first appear to us, are presumed always to be firmly placed in the here-and-now, always in the public (and thus contestable) domain. And so, what is said to be an identity (a noun, naming a seemingly static item) is no longer seen as the source but is always understood as the result of identity claims/acts and counter-claims/acts (verbs, signifying active processes). In this way, such mundane linguistic devices as "express yourself" may now be understood not as benign language or an innocently neutral description of how meaning works its way out of our heads and into the world beyond but, rather, as the Afterword makes clear, as themselves being curious techniques used to recreate the impression that personhood, or self, is a stable interior attribute manifested outwardly.

As venues where we could carry out this rethinking, the group developed two book series and a blog; one of those series – the one in which this volume appears (and edited by Vaia Touna) – is entitled *Working With Culture on the Edge* and is intentionally intertwined with the blog, inasmuch as the members of the group revise thematically related posts but then invite a set of new scholars to offer substantive responses to the pieces; in fact, "response" is not even a sufficient term since the ideal counterpoint to any of the main chapters that follow is hardly a reply but, instead, is an application, an expansion, a revision, even a critique, whereby the respondent takes the original piece as their beginning and thus the basis on which they can work to achieve something new, treating it as data even – all in hopes of further exploring the rethinking of identity that our group has set as our main task. Thus, the contents of this book are purposefully arranged in pairs. Moreover, while the members of Culture on the Edge are themselves at a variety of career phases, from tenure-track to full professorship, the respondents are all at rather earlier stages of their careers: largely, they're doctoral students (or at least were when they wrote the following chapters). This is also intentional on our part; for, given the number of scholars of religion who still go about their work as if those things classed as religion were somehow a special case, we find that it is a younger generation of scholars who share many of our own frustrations with this version of our field and so these are the people to whom many of us write. So what better group to invite along on this intellectual experiment, to see what might profitably be said about identity if we stop assuming the philosophically idealist inside-out model and, instead, take seriously the historicity of human subjects – which includes not just agents but also the settings to which they are inevitably subjugated.

For instance, consider a passage from Bayart which aims to press this very point: after quoting from Maria Iordanidu's novel, *Loxandra* (c. 1963) – a novel set in the early nineteenth century in the city then known as Constantinople – concerning an episode in which an otherwise unassuming shopkeeper is questioned by the protagonist as to whether he had participated in the massacre of Armenians, Bayart elaborates:

> The abruptness of this slide into mayhem, which shocks foreign observers, is surprising only because we take for granted the principle of identity-related uniqueness. Without being agreeable, it becomes plausible if we recognize that everyone is given to tinkering with his or her identity, depending on the alchemy of the circumstances. To that extent, the idea of community is debatable. It suggests too strongly that we belong to one, aggregate identity, which is supposed to dictate our interests and passions, whereas we tend to situate ourselves with respect to "a plurality of partially disjunctive, partially overlapping communities" [quoting the late Denys Lombard] – but then why should we keep using the term, if it is clearly misleading? It is not a matter of denying the terrible efficacy of identities that are felt to be primordial. Although we are convinced of the "artificial origin of the belief in common ethnicity," so we must acknowledge that this belief works, and that "rational association" is likely to be transformed into "personal relationships" in an "overarching communal

consciousness" [quoting Max Weber, the early twentieth-century German sociologist].

Bayart continues:

> In some sense, primordial identities "exist," but as mental facts and as regimes of subjectivity, not as structures. Instead of being explanatory factors, they must themselves be explained: while we agree that "identity, considered ethnographically, must always be mixed, relational, and inventive," that it is "conjunctural, not essential" [quoting James Clifford], it remains to be understood under what conditions a group of individuals apprehends it in the form of a permanent, primordial core in order to follow magicians who instrumentalise this illusion to their own advantage. (2005: 94–5)

To investigate this very point – how this thing we call identity comes to exist *as if* it is set apart and original – this little volume collects together a set of main pieces, in which members of our group each offer alternative ways of answering the seemingly simple question, "Who Are You?" thereby prompting them to reflect on one of their own many identities (whether national, gendered, racial, familial, professional, etc.), theorizing at the same time the self-identification that they each chose to discuss (examining the conditions and situations that might have brought it into being). Each is followed by a commentary that takes the main piece in an entirely new direction, seeing in it an opportunity to reflect even further on these operational acts of identification. And the volume ends with a longer reflection on just what this turn from the noun toward the verb might entail.

For it is our contention that *claiming* to be something, i.e., experiencing oneself as a certain sort of something and being treated by others as a member of a certain sort of group, does not prevent one from examining, and thereby making evident, the contingent devices and happenstance situations that made it possible to make such claims or to have such claims made about you. For inasmuch as we study the social life of human beings we are, sooner or later, our own data – making the things of which we write, in the following pieces, *as well as the very act of writing them*, curious artifacts that deserve our attention. And if such attention can then model for the interested reader an alternative approach to examining how it is that we navigate social life (an approach readers can apply in who knows what other situations) – or, better put, how social life navigates us! – then all the better. For, at the end of the day, that is what animates these little volumes: a pedagogical hope to provide but a few examples that might provoke in the reader a novel thought or two.

## Reference

Bayart, Jean-François (2005 [1996]). *The Illusion of Cultural Identity*. Trans. Steven Rendall et al. Chicago: The University of Chicago Press.

Russell T. McCutcheon is Professor and Chair of the Department of Religious Studies at the University of Alabama. He has published widely on the study of religion's history and the politics of classification – specifically the socio-political uses of the taxon "religion" (whether employed as a folk or technical term).

# 1. Who Are You? I'm a Religious Studies Scholar

## K. Merinda Simmons

The inevitable moment when people I meet for the first time ask what I do tends to be a bit of an awkward one. It goes something a little like this:

> "So, what do you do, Merinda?"
> "I'm a religious studies professor at the University of Alabama."
> "What sort of stuff do you work on?"
> "I'm interested in how and why people make authenticity claims…. I focus mostly on these claims in relation to gender, race, and the South."
> "…wait, but didn't you say you're in a religion department?"
> "Yeah."
> "So that's the kind of stuff you can study in a PhD program in religion?"
> "Well, sure! My PhD is in English though."

It's at this point that most people change the subject. But for those who act interested in how it happens that someone with an English degree is doing her teaching and research in a religious studies context, I try to explain the following….

One the one hand, no, I never expected that I'd wind up in a religious studies department. I didn't give much thought to "religious studies" at all, really. Like so many in my graduate cohort, I thought the name of the discipline was also the name of one's career path. Sure, people like talking about "interdisciplinary" scholarship, but even now, I find little consensus or clarity about what that term means. More often than not, it seems to refer to academic work that touches on a variety of topics, but not necessarily with any analytical consistency. In other words, one's methodology has an easy way of changing with one's respective object of study.

On the other hand, I think scholars make quite small our studies and interests when we reduce them to our datasets. If the academic study of religion is about having an ethnographic expertise in the history and language of this or that belief system, then sure, I'm no more a scholar of religion than I am of botany. But if the work we do as scholars of religion is to do with being curious about a taxonomic category (in this case "religion") – how it's used and by whom for what reasons – then I don't see how that's so different than using this or that novel or poem to look at the ways in which a trope like "masculinity" is utilized and contested, for instance. In either case, it isn't what the scholar is looking at that matters so much as the questions asked about it and the method(s) of inquiry used.

My theory seminars were always my favorite classes in graduate school, but it wasn't until I began writing my dissertation and had to choose the texts to which I'd direct my attention for the next couple of years that I really got the fact that it didn't ultimately matter what texts I chose. Sure, I had my favorites – the books I returned to again and again or found productively troubling – but that is expressly about my own tastes and what I like to read, not about the obvious texts to use in a particular strand of literary criticism. What's more, as I got further into the project and began making the rounds on the job market, I found a far easier and more accurate answer to the question of what I was writing to be about my approach rather than my topic. Some of the search committee members who interviewed me said bluntly this made me difficult "to place." Even when job ads mentioned interests in candidates with "critical approaches to gender" or training in postcolonial theory, I found quickly that many schools nonetheless were really looking for someone to fill the slot of a Shakespearean, or an Americanist, or a Chaucerian, etc. I wasn't all that surprised…. Nine ads out of every ten said as much.

This is too often the case for departments within the Humanities, as far as I'm concerned. Religious studies is no exception. As Aaron

Hughes and Randi Warne discuss in their *Bulletin for the Study of Religion* piece, "Death by Area Studies,"[1] departments are often looking to fill their ranks with area specialists. Academic disciplines thus go about the business of perpetuating their own authenticity claims, suggesting clearly knowable content relating to a certain time period, region, author, or what-have-you. But I was lucky. I met the folks working in the Department of Religious Studies at the University of Alabama.

Suddenly I was talking to people who pressed me on the how and why of my research interests rather than the what. We certainly don't all agree or have the same approach. But we do largely share a commitment to thinking seriously about methods and critical tools with which we approach our teaching and research. What that means for me personally is that I am able to extend my basic approach to authenticity and social order/power to all sorts of datasets without fear of stepping outside my disciplinary classification. What it also means is that, when people ask me what I do, I'm able to say, "I'm a religious studies scholar." Their confused responses are really what present the perfect moment to explain what it is I do: I think and write about how people resort to and rely on authenticity claims…, like those we make about disciplinary designation.

K. Merinda Simmons is Associate Professor of Religious Studies at the University of Alabama. She is editor of the Equinox series *Concepts in the Study of Religion: Critical Primers* and is currently working on a monograph tentatively entitled *Sourcing Slave Religion: Theorizing Experience in the American South* as well as two co-authored books: *Gender: A Critical Primer* (with Craig Martin) and *Race and New Modernisms* (with James A. Crank).

---

1 Posted at http://bulletin.equinoxpub.com/2014/11/death-by-area-studies/ (accessed July 15, 2016).

# 2.   Am I a Religious Studies Scholar?

**David G. Robertson**

I *am* a Religious Studies scholar…but I don't study "religion." Or that's what I'm told. At least, not *real* religion….

Robert Segal wrote that Religious Studies "does not require either a distinctive method or a distinctive explanation to be worthy of disciplinary status" (2006: xvii) – a quotation which has recently been circulating on social media again. There, it has generally been taken as both a justification of the field despite its ongoing and often impassioned definitional issues, and a call for "us" to put aside our (by implication) petty squabbles and get on with the serious matter of Studying Religion. (Why I have put "us" in quotations should, I hope, be clear by the end of the piece.) While I share Segal's concern over the boundaries of the discipline, he's quite right, of course – to be an academic field, Religious Studies just needs people to assert that it is. Once there are a few people with jobs, the field will begin to defend itself. The historical fact that alchemy or astrology have at some point been considered legitimate disciplines, later to become "rejected knowledge" (Barkun 2003), should not discourage us. The structures of knowledge change, we know this.

But in asserting that Religious Studies is among the area studies, rather than a field, I'm concerned that we're tacitly admitting that RS scholars know *implicitly* what Religion is, even if they admit we can't quite define it. This bothers me – for what defines the area? I'm sure that it goes without saying (in this volume at least) that it is not the job of RS scholars to argue *for* Religion, to advocate for its importance or relevance, as though it was a social entity with a necessary but oppressed role in society. Rather, the task is to problematize "religion" as a category, to challenge the taken-for-grantedness of the term, and to historicize its usage. That said, I doubt that the question of definition matters to many beyond two groups: the religious, and those who make their living research-ing them. I hate to tell you this, but the general public don't care. Mostly, they don't even know what we do.

But I am getting ahead of myself. I took my degree, my masters and my doctorate in Religious Studies, all in the School of Divinity of the University of Edinburgh in the UK. I started off interested in New Testament studies, but was always drawn to the weirder bits – e.g., Gnosticism, Apocalypse and heresies of all sorts. As time wore on, I found myself increasingly drawn to popular modern uses of these ideas, and thus became interested in alternative religions and the New Age milieu. After reading more into the academic work, I was struck by the prevalence of conspiracy theories in that milieu, and became puzzled that no one was looking seriously at them, despite the obvious and poignant theoretical parallels with the study of religions (I'll get to that in due course).[1] Even so, and despite the support and encouragement of open-minded, theoretically and empirically focused scholars (like Stephen Sutcliffe and James Cox), my undergraduate dissertation on the subject was practically dismissed by an internal examiner. So glaring was the difference between the internal and external examiners (and our interests) that, unusually, a third opinion was sought. Thankfully, I passed, but this was not the only time my work would be dismissed in this way.

In the 1970s, scholars doing the kind of work I do were the hot ticket. Even though stats that support those who are for the decline of traditional forms of religious identification and practice are now larger than they were back then, secularization (the assumption that religion would inevitably become irrelevant) was then the dominant narrative. Popular new religions could challenge that narrative, or confirm it, depending on how you looked at the data. But some-thing shifted in the late 1990s, and the traditional religions again

---

1 There were other scholars, many of whom I have been privileged to work with since, but I didn't know that at the time. I was younger and naive.

became prominent in the media and in political rhetoric. Nowadays, the academy seems only to want people working in interfaith studies or the crypto-theological field known as Material Religion (studying religion via the examination of objects). The market leads, as in all things.

At a recent job interview, one on the panel looked at my CV and said, "You don't even have a tradition, do you?" I replied that in terms of sheer numbers, popular beliefs like reincarnation or UFOs or conspiracy theories have more proponents than some of the more "acceptable" traditions. For example, only 1 percent of the US population are Muslim, but according to a 2013 Public Policy Polling survey, 4 percent believe that reptilian extraterrestrials walk among us.[2] Forty-six percent of the UK population identify as Christian, but 30 percent believe in ghosts.[3] I wasn't surprised that this comment fell on deaf ears. I was rather concerned, however, that my own religious identification (or more accurately, lack thereof) was being critiqued.

I was also privileged to take James Cox's course based on his then-forthcoming *From Primitive to Indigenous* (2007), which I still consider an important contribution to the critical reappraisal of the World Religion Paradigm. In all honesty, I had little-to-no interest in indigenous religions, but Cox is an engaging and subtly persuasive teacher. By taking the development of the academic study of "primitive," "primal," or "indigenous" religions as subject matter, the course triggered in me an interest in theory and disciplinary formation that continues to this day. Applying his critique of "Indigenous religion" to the contemporary scene, I became more and more interested in the boundary work being done. Why are certain versions of rationality set apart by scholars (and seen as legitimate or not), but not others? Why wasn't New Age *really* religion? Why did its commodification mean it was superficial? Why did its construction from

2 http://www.publicpolicypolling.com/main/2013/04/conspiracy-theory-poll-results-.html (accessed July 7, 2016).

3 https://yougov.co.uk/news/2016/03/26/o-we-of-little-faith/ (accessed July 7, 2016).

diverse sources mean its subscribers shouldn't be taken seriously? It was clear to me that implicit – and, typically, essentialist – models of religion were not only dominant, but were being aggressively defended by people with "a horse in the race."

In short, I was becoming a critical scholar.

And so I found myself triply marginal – studying data which is not really religion, combined with conspiracies which are beyond contempt, and to make it worse, I was being critical about the whole endeavor.

But what does any of this have to do with identity? Well, two things, actually.

Firstly, after all, if "religion" is *not* an utterly unique "thing in itself" – a claim that I have no doubt would be supported by all the contributors to this volume – but is, instead, a complex nexus of cultural currents with a particular history and context emerging from the colonial project, then observing these dynamics elsewhere (in things not usually called religions) will help us to understand this process. If so, then how are categories such as "conspiracy theory," for example, being constructed and mobilized by interested parties? This is, of course, one of the central tenets of the critical project – how knowledge is defined by particular interests. Why are certain versions of these dynamics set apart, and others ignored, or even stigmatized? After all, there is nothing *intrinsically* more ridiculous or untrue about the claims of Scientology founder L. Ron Hubbard or British conspiracist David Icke than the claims of Christian or Muslim or African indigenous religion leaders. We are simply much less used to hearing them. Yet the polemics we encounter frequently in work on new religions and conspiracy theories (less overtly in the former but still explicitly and aggressively in the latter) never take into account that some 80 percent of the US population subscribe to ideas which are just as immune to scientific investigation as the idea that reptilians walk among us. Yet only one of these ideas is creating jobs in RS departments, while the other is simply dismissed as irrelevant, outside our field, or even beneath us. If some ideas may be tolerated, with the addition of qualifiers to make it clear they're a marginal concern ("New," "Indigenous," etc.) then why are other acts and ideas which can easily be included in the rubric "religion" set apart and denied further investigation? Especially when, in terms of sheer numbers, such popular views may have *more* support than the "real religions"?

Second, I feel strongly that, as Russell McCutcheon puts it in the introduction to this volume, "our tools are applicable far more widely than just the study of religion." Indeed, without being trained in methodological agnosticism – the approach that avoids asking normative questions – I may not have been able to study such "deviant" worldviews as conspiracy theories with an even hand. But in doing so, I have come to see that the comparative project is not so agnostic, after all. For who decides which worldviews we are permitted to compare? Ninian Smart's admonition that we should consider worldviews equally has not been carried through – not that Smart really believed it anyway. The fact is, the things we are allowed to study under the rubric "religion" are those which support the agenda of liberal theology. So they support an agenda of Western "modern" morality, of "faith," with women and other minorities now "included." We study things that are peaceful. And scholarship slips into "interfaith" and other forms of implicit statecraft, RS becoming another of what Louis Althusser would term an Ideological State Apparatus (ISA). Increasingly, RS departments' faculties are made up of representatives of each of the Big Five World Religions, frequently people for whom the boundary between their professional field and their personal identification is, to say the least, unclear. How can one be expected to critique a category in which one is implicated? As Timothy Fitzgerald states:

> religious studies is an agency for uncritically formulating and legitimating this myth and embedding it into the warp and woof of our collective consciousness – a modern ideological category transformed by ritual repetition such that it seems as though it is in the nature of things. (2007: 9–10)

Fitzgerald has described the contemporary study of religion as a continuation of the medieval discourse on civility and barbarity. I suggest that study of conspiracy narratives – and their almost-complete marginalization by the academy – is an even clearer example. There are certain things of which it is permitted to consider, and others of which we are not permitted to speak. So those who claim to be merely describing religion are deeply involved in maintaining the category, if only in allowing us to consider those things that fit implicit ideas of what religion is.

(An aside: Can you imagine a social scientist who was as openly an advocate of conspiracy theories as many religious studies scholars are of their religious and or ethnic backgrounds? And no, Noam Chomsky doesn't count.)[4]

So, to return to where we began, who is the "we" Segal refers to? Those of us who already know what Religion is, and merely want to chart its ever more diverse unfoldings throughout history? Or those of us who seek to chart the uses (but not "abuses") of a broad but politically and socially powerful term? I count myself in the latter group, but I am increasingly uncertain if members of that group are included within the field known as Religious Studies.

As scholars we like to think that we simply become interested in certain things, but in truth we create and defend disciplines. And we do this to a large degree through what we deign to include in the category. Identifying something as (a) religion – with or without some qualifier like "Indigenous" or "New" stuck in front of it to remind us that it's not one of the Big Five – legitimizes it. Ask yourself: Why doesn't the academy call New Religious Movements simply New Religions? Or for that matter, simply, Religions? The answer is plain: because it would give the impression that these were equally valid as the World Religions. The terminology which defines the field – if only implicitly – protects its members from criticism, and makes the category a subject of which serious talk is permitted. So when we name our discipline as "Religious Studies" and not, say, "the bizarre ideas of some foreigners," we are constructing the very object that we ought to be committed to critiquing.

---

4 He's a linguist, for one, and also critical of most conspiracy narratives, and those who adhere to them.

So, yes, I don't have a job yet – but neither does Timothy Fitzgerald (anymore). Isn't it curious that one of the most fervent critics of the category finds himself out of work at a time when 50 percent of job adverts ask for Islam as a speciality? Now I sound conspiratorial....

I for one care not a jot if Religious Studies continues to exist as a field, or is absorbed into other departments (as sometimes happens, here in the UK or in North America). I could continue my research into the epistemically marginal anywhere, though I suspect other departments would be just as dismissive. But I know that the Big Five will keep Religious Studies departments going as long as they can. The public and the media will continue to ignore the work being done. And they will care little if the views of millions who buy homeopathic remedies, tarot readings, Angel color cards, crystals and dreamcatchers are included.

After all, it's not really Religion, is it?

# References

Barkun, Michael (2003). *A Culture of Conspiracy: Apocalyptic Visions in Contemporary America*. Berkeley, CA: University of California Press. https://doi.org/10.1525/california/9780520238053.001.0001

Cox, James L. (2007). *From Primitive to Indigenous: The Academic Study of Indigenous Religions*. Aldershot, UK: Ashgate.

Fitzgerald, Timothy (2007). *Discourse on Civility and Barbarity: A Critical History of Religion and Related Categories*. New York: Oxford University Press.

Segal, Robert A. (2006). "Introduction." In Robert A. Segal, ed., *The Blackwell Companion to the Study of Religion*. Malden, UK: Blackwell.

David G. Robertson holds a PhD in Religious Studies from the University of Edinburgh. His research examines connections between conspiracist and millennial ideas, as well as spiritualities and popular culture. He is also founding editor and podcast co-host of The Religious Studies Project, co-editor of the journal *Implicit Religion*, and a committee member of the British Association for the Study of Religions.

# 3. Who Are You? I'm Wednesday's Child

## Craig Martin

Identities are weird things. Presumably, telling you my identity lets you draw up associations and predictions about me and my behavior based on that identity, as well as sympathies or antipathies, depending perhaps on whether or not you share the identity at hand. For instance, if I told you I am a Republican, you might additionally assume that I'm probably either socially or fiscally conservative, that I'm not a fan of Barack Obama, etc. – and, depending on how you identify, you might see me as on your side (someone to whom you should extend the benefit of the doubt) or as an opponent (toward whom you needn't feel any sympathies). So here goes: I was a Wednesday baby. That's right – I was born on a Wednesday. Crazy, right? I'm one of *them*.

Too random, perhaps? It's an arbitrary point from which you can't draw any conclusions about me? Would you prefer to know how much melanin I have in my body? The longitude and latitude coordinates of my birth? How many times I've circled the sun? Maybe the amount of melanin can tell you whether I'm liable to prefer rock or hip hop? Maybe the latitude and longitude of my birth can tell you whether I'm a brash like an American or reserved like a Brit? Maybe from the number of times I've circled the sun you could figure out if I'm likely to be loyal to my employer like a baby boomer or distrustful of authority like a Gen Xer? Could you draw out some behavioral predictions from those things? Are the amount of melanin in my body, the latitude and longitude of my birth, or the number of times I've circled the sun any less random than the day of the week on which I was born?

The last case – which generation do I belong to? – is perhaps the most interesting. According to some estimates, there are upwards of 80 million "millennials" in the United States – the generation born after 1980. They make up about 25 percent of the total population. Interestingly, the size of such a massive group doesn't prevent journalists – and sometimes academics – from making broad, sweeping claims about the group as a whole. For instance, there is a *widespread* assumption that millennials enter the job market with a great deal of entitlement (notably, my Google search for "millennials entitlement" turned up 145,000 results). By contrast, there are a little more than 40 million who identify as African-American in the US, making up less than 15 percent of the total population. Most journalists wouldn't dare make sweeping generalizations about all African-Americans – at least not openly – and yet apparently have no qualms when making such generalizations about a group twice the size.

Oddly, the fact that I "know" that such generalizations are problematic doesn't stop my brain from drawing up these identifications and their associated narratives. There are apparently about 65 million Gen Xers in the US (according to how the Pew Research Center divides up the generations, Gen X includes those born between 1965 and 1980), and I implicitly and explicitly identify with them. According to the popular narrative, we are slackers and latchkey kids who grew up watching MTV, highly skeptical of authority, not particularly loyal to our workplace because we saw our parent's loyalty go unrewarded, and we love to sneer at the millennials who all got participation trophies growing up. With my confirmation bias firmly in hand, I see myself in this narrative. I too was a latchkey kid, I taped the Pearl Jam episode of MTV Unplugged and watched it over and over, I had a crush on Janeane Garofalo, I have a chip on my shoulder about "the man," and I often wonder why millennials can't see that it's impossible for everyone to be above average.

Upon further reflection, however, the narrative starts to look questionable. Yes, I was the kid who collected CDs of all the bands that came out of Seattle between 1991 and '94 – including five or eight Sub Pop Mudhoney releases – but I was only a latchkey kid for part of my youth, I am greatly deferential to many forms of authority (and wield it myself), and frequently find myself defending millennials against the charge that they're entitled. Perhaps there's little relation between the Gen X narrative and my life experience other than my elective affinity. And yet, I still *enjoy* identifying as a Gen Xer, and gain some sense of satisfaction from it.

I'm uncertain of the consequences of this act of identification. It is most likely biased along the lines of class and race. I suspect few African-American "Gen Xers" have the same sort of nostalgia over Doc Martens as I. I doubt the "Gen Xers" in the 1 percent are disloyal to their workplace because they probably own the workplace (note: the 1 percent and the 99 percent are also interesting categories that allow us to draw out all sorts of questionable associations like I just did there). One wonders what the effects are of a set of associations thrown onto an entire generation when they're based on a white and middle-class picture.

Craig Martin is an Associate Professor of Religious Studies at St. Thomas Aquinas College. His research focuses on questions of theory and method in the study of religion, and his recent works include *A Critical Introduction to the Study of Religion* (2012) and *Capitalizing Religion: Ideology and the Opiate of the Bourgeoisie* (2014).

# 4. Seeing the Forest *and* the Trees

## Sarah Levine

"Are the amount of melanin in my body, the latitude and longitude of my birth, or the number of times I've circled the sun any less random than the day of the week on which I was born?" asks Craig Martin. If we think imaginatively, it's possible to agree with his observation that "these facts are not any more or less random than any other about ourselves." But in reality – that is, in the practice of our everyday lives and in social space – the question belies a more complicated situation. Anyone who's lived in a society that privileges one race over others, one gender over others, a particular age range over others, a socioeconomic status over others, a religion over others, knows that living these facts isn't an arbitrary experience. They are, we can all agree, historical. They become embedded over generations and centuries, so that acts of identification are choices under varying constraints and with conflicting allegiances.

Our identities are created *in situ* by our *own* "operational acts of identification," (for instance, the collection – and no doubt display – of albums and mixtapes released by the best and just mediocre bands of the Pacific Northwest's '90s), but they are also formed by our own acts performed as *resistance* to identification, and, importantly, by the acts and discriminatory behaviors of others. The sociological critique of culture is an important intervention in how we understand our political, social, religious, and aesthetic affiliations. But theorizing identity construction should be a fragile practice and one undertaken not to merely disrupt the status quo or to shock a bolt of objectivity into our critiques. I take Martin's essay as an invitation to speak about one of my own identity affiliations as a Jewish

American. Religio-ethnic identity may seem a deal "weightier" than generational identity, but then again, is one of these, as Martin asks, any more random than the other?

When I was eight years old, my father sat me down in our living room and together we watched Steven Spielberg's 1993 film *Schindler's List*. It must have been some time in spring because I recall our viewing coinciding with the annual Yom HaShoah, Holocaust Remembrance Day. We watched that film together, and the experience remains emblematic of my relationship with him, one in which he respected a maturity and understanding that I perhaps did not have, and one that felt grounded in the reinforcement of ties to our Jewish identity. It was with him that I went to weekly Torah study, it was with him that I rehearsed Hebrew, and it was through him that I learned how important Israel was in his, and therefore, my, psyche.

Even in a Reform community, *being Jewish* was a defining characteristic growing up. In my Jewish preschool I practiced being an *emah* (mother) on Friday afternoons when my teachers led the girls in lighting the Sabbath candles and ushering the light inward with our hands before covering our faces and reciting the Sabbath prayer. When my family moved to a Bible-belt suburb of Atlanta just before I began kindergarten, I learned almost immediately, and repeatedly, that my being Jewish wasn't just how things were, but that it was something I needed to be guarded about. Before summer was over, a new friend who lived up the street told me I was going to hell. I had never heard of the place, but her tone made it clear that I should be scared. It was the first among many times that I was damned by friends and classmates. I was terrified of other kids' parents, who somehow, I figured, came to hate my family and me without ever speaking to us, and made sure, through their children, that I knew as much.

Over time, however, I was able to adapt to the exclusion, to develop a pride of difference. I leaned into Judaism, attending synagogue three times a week for religious school, Sabbath services followed by Torah study, and Hebrew school, and I became invested in the stories of the Hebrew Bible. This ancient tradition was full of dramatic sagas of human achievement, capitulation, failure, and redemption. Characters like King David and Sarah and Vashti and Joseph were fascinating studies in human complexity. I began to investigate how to win theological arguments that had left me speechless and afraid as a child, and I girded myself in defense against attacks from my committed but combative Christian class-mates. For the most part, I was able to ignore some of the more extreme Chosen People talk that didn't capture my imagination: the increasing number of reminders, as I got older, that I needed to marry a Jewish man; the teaching that having Jewish children was my responsibility to my people; the singing of the Israeli national anthem at the end of every single religious service.

My dad died suddenly a month after my Bat Mitzvah, and both events happened to trigger my induction into American teenage life. My poor and amazing mother was the sole recipient of my teen-age-girl angst and wrath while my father took on legendary propor-tions of greatness. For example, I knew that in 1966, when he was a nineteen-year-old idealist, he moved to Israel for a year where he milked cows on a kibbutz. It became, I think, a mythic time in his own life, and it certainly became a story of outsized proportion in my own conception of my father, who – you have to understand – was much of *my world*. He was there during the 1967 war, and that experience seems to have solidified what became a total, unwaver-ing support for Israel. Idealistic utopias, it turns out, had to resort to violence at least some of the time. The Promised Land was delivered out of myth and into political reality, and I know he tried to teach my brother and me from the time we were very young that it's part of the Jewish responsibility to make sure Israel's continued existence is secured. The fact of the Holocaust, and our redemption in Israel, was both the prime mover and silent framework by which he taught us to understand Judaism, and in fact, considerations of "Judaism" prior to the Second World War remain an intellectual obstacle for me.

That the Holocaust and the subsequent establishment of Israel is foundational for American Jewry isn't a new observation, but it's something that, if you come from a secularized but practicing

Jewish family, you learn individually and slowly over time. As *religious* practice became less important in my life, as it does for many adults, Jewish *political* commitments emerged as the prominent feature of Jewish identity. And yet, this sort of Jewish being never truly resonated with me. Despite my father's insistence, I don't feel any more connected to the Holocaust than I imagine most of humanity does when confronted with its atrocity, and as a result, I am ambivalent about the nationhood of Israel. It was in college that I began to dis-identify with Judaism; it began mildly with piercings and tattoos (a flagrant rebuke of Jewish Law, and also a ritual induction to a different community) and, ultimately, culminated when my initial ambivalence about Israel turned to deep ethical discomfort with the state and the moralized arguments that underpinned its creation and sustain its policies regarding the expansion of Jewish settlements and discrimination against Jews of African descent.

I am not alone in these feelings. As history moves further in time away from the Holocaust, Jewish identity has splintered and multiplied around the meaning of the Holocaust and Israel in Jewish history. Where my father and grandfather (who, it must be noted, witnessed the horror of Nazi terror as he liberated concentration camps as an American soldier during World War II) could not imagine Judaism without the Holocaust and its redemption, the modern state of Israel, my commitment to this narrative is more precarious. At this distance, Israel is more complicated than salvific; its creation and maintenance, in a toxic paradigm of unyielding pain and fear, colonization, war, and ethno-nationalism, implicates us (it is a *Jewish* state, after all) in abuses of power and privilege. But on this point, i.e., modern Judaism's North Star, I feel alienated from much of my immediate Jewish community and from my family.

And yet, I wonder, what does it mean that these considerations hold such psychological power over me? Is my ethical critique of Israel a product of being Jewish or, perhaps, something else entirely, such as being a humanist? I certainly don't extend my most biting opprobrium to other nations, some of which act far more inhumanely. And what does it mean that I goad my Jewish family into these arguments? Is it to antagonize them as part of a larger and complicated family dynamic or is it an act of mourning, a way of trying to engage in a conversation that I never had an opportunity to have with my father?

Even as American Jews are freer now more than ever to assimilate or dissociate from traditional forms of Jewish life, I recall that this was not always the case. In the not-too-distant past, the assimilation, universalism, and cosmopolitanism practiced by ethnic Jews were seen not merely as anti-nationalist customs at odds with Nazi ideology, but as the embodiment of a sinister and conspiratorial being. Ironically, now it is much of modern American Judaism that cautions against embracing too eagerly these freedoms. Our existence is one *as a people*, different and distinct from others, banded together by a religious covenant, a cultural responsibility, and a secular nationalism. Thinking too much about this is psychologically paralyzing, and my allegiance to this identity feels at times both incredibly meaningful and woefully meaningless.

As might be expected from the above narrative, I don't perform much identifiable Judaism anymore. I don't attend synagogue; I don't participate in exclusive Jewish social activities; I have no plans to marry, let alone marry a Jewish man and have children; I certainly don't donate to AIPAC (the American Israel Public Affairs Committee). Nevertheless, the concept of Judaism, its evolutionary paths, and my questionable place in their narratives still occupies much of my mental space and self-consideration. I *feel* a bond, an ever tenuous rootedness, even if it can't be seen.

An ongoing debate in the humanities and social sciences remains whether we can study anything below the surface, *or if there exists anything but surface*. Quieter complexities feel like they're boiling behind our everyday elective affiliations and shorthand identities. Psychologies, family history, childhood memories, ancient animations. They are difficult to study, and there are strong arguments that because of their mutability and susceptibility to self-serving narratives, they shouldn't be the object of a scholar's study. What they do reveal, however, is that some identities are anything but random.

Sarah Levine is the associate director of publishing at the American Academy of Religion, where she is the managing editor of *Religious Studies News*. She received her MA in Religious Studies from Georgia State University in 2012, and her areas of interest include aesthetics, performance, and the constructive boundaries of art and religion as well as academic labor justice, the business of higher education, and digital scholarship.

# 5.  Who Are You? I'm Greek

## Vaia Touna

Although we all have many identities, the first thing that I want to mention now, when I meet someone, is my national identity. This of course has to do with the fact that I have been living, the last five years, away from my country, that is, Greece. So, yes, I'm Greek! To remember the first time you realized you were of a certain nationality is not that easy. Of course I know, because I have been told many times by my parents, that I was born in Athens; this is not an insignificant detail for me because Athens is, after all, the capital of Greece, but also because while growing up I learned how important Athens has been through the ages – well ok, mainly, in the Classical period (that is, fifth century BCE) and the Golden age of Pericles – which made, in my mind, my origins tale a bit more glamorous. Now, although I was born in Athens, I didn't grow up there; the city I can recall and which is the city where I grew up is Thessaloniki, the second-largest city in Greece, and which you might also hear referenced as the country's co-capital (how many countries do you know that have co-capitals? Well, we are unique that way, ha!). I have to admit that, depending on circumstances, I would either stress my Athenian origin or I would completely ignore it and focus on Thessaloniki.

Anyway, the fact is that it fills me with pride when I'm asked to show someone around Thessaloniki or even to talk about my ancient Greek heritage, which I see is of great interest to my North American friends. Of course this pride has its ups and downs, especially when I'm asked about the current politico-economic situation in Greece, but even that becomes a moment to distinguish my Greek identity from a European identity (but maybe that's for another essay); the point here is, what is being Greek or, maybe better, how do I know I'm one?

Being Greek is many things but let us start from the beginning: it means that your ancestors (I won't go as far as to say my great-great-grandparents, but, well...) were Homer, Socrates, Plato, Aristotle, and Alexander the Great, and many others of course. Growing up in Greece you spend your primary and secondary school years learning about those ancient ancestors and in the end they are not only more familiar than modern Greek philosophers or even politicians, but they're also the ideal to which everything and everyone is compared. Now, of course, I (and I'm sure others like me) could write all sorts of stories of how, when I was at school learning about my ancient history, I could more easily identify myself with the democratic Athenians rather than the militaristic Spartans, especially during the Peloponnesian War (431–404 BCE) – besides, the Golden Age of Pericles had a glamor of its own (no wonder fifth-century Athens became my scholarly interest) – but I was with the Spartans when we (or should I say *they*?) fought against the Persians in the battle of Thermopylae, in 480 BCE (though, of course, the way the story is told by Herodotus, it was not just Spartans who fought the Persians but a "Greek alliance"). And of course learning, or better being schooled, also about Macedonians, Philip II, and his son Alexander the Great, played a significant role in understanding what it is to be Greek, because the Macedonians (Thessaloniki is in that area) did what the egocentric Athenians failed to do: unite us all, unite the Greeks! The story of how the Roman Empire took us over was never my favorite, and it was somehow downplayed, as far as I can recall, in school, but Byzantium and Constantine the Great soon made things better – that is, until the Turks came and we spent the next 400 years under "the Turkish yoke," until the 1821 revolution against them. This is when the Modern Greek state emerged, and from Greeks (Hellenes) we became New Greeks (Neo-Hellenes).[1]

---

1  I hope you are following in this narration my use of personal pronouns.

I can easily say "I'm Greek" but it's less easy to start explaining as to *how* or *when* I came about being self-aware that I am one, though my school years (as you can tell) certainly helped towards that. History, whether in schools or not, I suppose, has that effect; through the telling of stories, both of victories and glorious moments as well as of defeats and losses, a certain identity is evoked and strengthened in the telling and retelling. Or as Willi Braun wrote:

> "History," thus, whatever else it is, is also a discursive means of social formation and contestation. This is why it is not surprising, for example, that the emergence of strong nationalist interests goes hand in hand with scrutinizing and tinkering with the history curricula in the schools...and passionate references to "the past," a past that may be substantively vague in popular memory, but that is rhetorically evocative nonetheless. (Braun 1999: 5)

But telling stories is one way in which one's own identity is formed and reformed, while acting is another, that is, the performance of the stories being taught. How many of you, I wonder, have participated in school celebrations where you had to act out a part that evoked a moment of your nation's history? Well, I certainly remember several such occasions. So, the first recollection I have of how important it is to be Greek goes back into my very early days in school; now, of course I don't really recall, but luckily pictures (our modern artifacts) help towards that direction. In this one picture that I have in mind I'm dressed like a Souliotopoula (a girl from Souli),[2] that is, I'm wearing a long white dress, an apron, a sleeveless black coat and a headscarf, and of course I am holding the Greek flag; it's not insignificant that this folklore costume, which represented the period when Greece was under the Ottoman rule, was handmade

---

2 Folklore stories talk about how, sometime in the eighteenth century, the women of Souli, an area in Epirus, that is located in the northwest part of Greece which is today near the border with Albania, decided to jump off, together with their children, from a cliff, dancing and singing, instead of surrendering to the local Ottoman ruler, Ali Pasha.

by my mom. Many times I've been told, by family members, that in this picture I was six years old and that we celebrated the 25th of March in Kindergarten, which is Greece's National Celebration of the 1821 revolution against the 400 years of slavery under the Ottoman Empire (that's how we would refer to it). Apparently, it was a big day for the family (and for me, I guess) because it was the first time that I was performing in a school's celebration, having to recite the following poem:

> Είμαι μια Ελληνοπούλα
> Και σαν μια Σουλιοτοπούλα
> Αγαπώ με την καρδία μου
> Την πατρίδα τη γλυκιά μου
> Κι εχθρός αν έρθει πάλι
> Με σκοπό να την προσβάλλει
> ΟΧΙ δεν θα τον αφήσω
> Και θα του φωνάξω πίσω.[3]

I don't really remember how reciting the poem made me feel (there's no picture for that), that is, whether I had a consciousness of my Greekness, but the reaction of my family that gathered for the kindergarten's celebration must have made me think that being Greek, whatever that means in the mentality of a six-year-old, and reciting as well as performing – by wearing the "right clothes" – that poem (which to this day I can remember not only the words but how I raised my hand when I said certain words from the poem, like "NO" and "Go Back") rather than just reading it, was very

3  I am a Greek
    And like a Souliotopoula
    I love with all my heart
    My sweet country
    And if an enemy comes again
    With intention to attack her*
    NO I will not let him*
    And I will shout "Go Back.
  * In Greek grammar "Greece" (the noun) is female and "enemy" (the noun) is male.

important. But now, wait a minute, whose past were we talking about, mine or theirs…?

So, to the opening question, "Who Are You?" the seemingly simple answer, "I'm Greek," appears to be a bit more complicated, especially in relation to the question of how *I* know *I'm* Greek. Because one would do well to pay attention to, if not to question, that personal pronoun; it should be evident from the above, some-how random choice of past events, that my recollection of what it means to be Greek was not mine to begin with but that of my parents, my school, my extended family; it was a reflection of how they all thought I ought to feel, repeatedly telling me. This eventually had the effect of my internalizing those feelings and ideas as if they have always been mine.

# Reference

Braun, Willi (1999). "Amnesia in the Production of (Christian) History." *Bulletin of the Council of Societies For the Study of Religion* 28(1): 3–9.

Vaia Touna is Assistant Professor at the Department of Religious Studies at the University of Alabama. Her interests range widely, from looking at spe-cific concepts of religion in the Greco-Roman world and methodological issues concerning the study of religion in general, to focusing on processes of identification with examples drawn from Ancient and Modern Greece. She is now working on a book tentatively titled *Fabrication of the Greek Past: Religion, Tradition, and Modern Identities.*

# 6. You're Greek? Well...,
# I'm (Northern) Irish, Kinda...

## Christopher R. Cotter

No man, no madness
Though their sad power may prevail
Can possess, conquer, my country's heart
They rise to fail
She is eternal
Long before nations' lines were drawn
When no flags flew, when no armies stood
My land was born
And you ask me why I love her
Through wars, death and despair
She is the constant, we who don't care
And you wonder will I leave her, but how?
I cross over borders but I'm still there now
How can I leave her?
Where would I start?
Let man's petty nations tear themselves apart
My land's only borders lie around my heart
(Rice, Andersson, and Ulvaeus 1986: 62–4)

In May 2016 I embarked on the short flight from Edinburgh
(Scotland) to Belfast (Northern Ireland) to sing in a farewell concert for the retiring Head of Music at my secondary school. The
final item on the emotionally charged program that evening was an
arrangement of "Anthem" from the musical *Chess* (quoted above)
which speaks wonderfully to themes of authenticity, timelessness,
and subjectivity hinted at in Vaia Touna's essay, and explored below.
Contributing further to my argument, the maestro introduced the

piece by suggesting that it should be "our" (Northern Ireland's? the UK's?) national anthem rather than the incredibly dull "God Save the Queen," presumably because the latter is particularly divisive in a Northern Irish context. I'll nod to "Anthem" throughout this essay, in which I reflect on the contextual tactics of identification from my own position as a (Northern) Irishman (these parentheses are important) who's been living in Edinburgh since 2004.

This isn't the place to provide a history of Northern Ireland – for that see Liechty and Clegg (2000), McGarry and O'Leary (1995), Mulholland (2003), Ruane and Todd (1996)[1] – yet my assumption is that the majority of my readers will know comparatively little of this, except for perhaps being aware that it's mired in a conflict tied to the identifications "Protestant" and "Catholic" (William of Orange, Battle of the Boyne, etc.), that at some point Ireland was partitioned into what are now known as the Republic of Ireland (an independent sovereign state) and Northern Ireland (a constituent unit – along with England, Wales and Scotland – of the United Kingdom of Great Britain and Northern Ireland). With this single sentence, we now share what I've *retrospectively* come to understand as the sum total of Northern Irish history that I brought with me to Edinburgh. While Touna can recall taking part in school celebrations acting out moments in her nation's history, I cannot even recall learning about my nation's history. I remember learning about the nineteenth-century "Great" or "Potato" Famine, and about the First World War..., but that's it. And people wonder why there are still tensions in Northern Ireland?

This *constructed* narrative is augmented with various memories from my childhood, growing up in what I'd *now* describe as a middle-class, Protestant (regularly attending the Anglican Church of Ireland) household. Throughout my life, I've been aware of the negatives: I've heard of the various murders, beatings, and bombs associated with the sectarian divide, seen the burning wreckage in the aftermath of each year's "marching season," and felt threatened

---

1 My own lack of literacy in (Northern) Irish history is one of the key points of this essay. Thanks to Gladys Ganiel for advice on these sources.

by the claims on territory marked by flags, painted kerbstones, and the like. I remember being baffled that so many of my primary school classmates *nominally* supported the Glasgow Rangers (known locally as simply Rangers),[2] and being teased for supporting Manchester United in the English Premier League, as they were dubbed Manchester's "taigy" team.[3] That I didn't yet understand the identifications that were taking place in all this, nor the meanings attached to the terms invoked, did nothing to diminish the feeling of being *othered*. More positively, it fills me with pride that the households in the suburban cul-de-sac we moved to in the mid-'90s were around fifty-fifty Catholic-Protestant (significantly, this was *common knowledge*), although my friends and I had to take extra care to downplay certain friends' "Irish" names when crossing the bridge to shop in the nearby "loyalist" estate.

But let's pause for a moment. For these snapshots are being presented from a very specific position, that's been fabricated over a number of years, and which fits with my current self-image of being "above this sort of thing." Much as the phrase "I'd never heard about Islam until 9/11" makes a potentially interesting story out of a gap in my memory, I have no idea whether (Northern) Irish history was largely absent from my schooling or not. My *assumption* now is that this material was too politically charged then to be included in school curricula, and that my parents' desire to keep me away from sectarianism necessitated a dearth of national identity formation at home. Similarly, I assume(d) that my classmates were claiming to support the Rangers for reasons other than their footballing prowess (most likely due to parental encouragement). But how do I know? All that I know for certain is that I was aware of the importance of identity politics when growing up, and had my own *tactics* for navigating day-to-day interactions.

---

2 A football club associated with the Protestant side of the sectarian divide. My assumption was that my classmates couldn't possibly really support Rangers, as Scottish football didn't seem to be (still isn't?) held in particularly high regard.

3 "Taig" is a derogatory term for a Catholic or Irish nationalist.

For example, one incident I remember with much fondness occurred during a 2003 stay in Normandy (France), where the friendly *gîte* (a vacation rental home) owner habitually raised the national flag of her guests on her garden flagpole. Not appreciating that my family were *"Northern* Irish," she'd raised the Republic of Ireland flag in our honor. Upon learning of her error (I've forgotten the particular circumstances, but I assume this was a jovial incident) she proceeded to raise the Union flag on the same pole. Given that this was possibly the first time in my life that I'd seen these two flags – each associated with violence, bigotry, and claims to terri-tory – flying side-by-side, I couldn't resist taking a picture, which subsequently became my profile picture on the then-popular MSN Messenger. Here my memories turn sour as I recollect an altercation with an acquaintance who demanded that I change my profile pic-ture: she'd rather die before she saw the "Union Jack" flying below a "Tricolour." I asked what bothered her so much, and she responded that the image was offensive to her religion which, it turned out, was "Protestant." I inquired further as to whether she attended church, and when she answered in the negative I rested my case, victorious. Just as I'd already concluded that my Rangers-supporting class-mates weren't "real" fans, she wasn't a "real" Protestant, but was simply *using* the word to mean "loyalist," and a bigoted one at that. This exemplifies the rhetoric of authenticity (Hughes 2015: xv) that is dominant in public discourse about religion, where "the operative assumption seems to be that 'religion' or a 'religious tradition' must be essentially good and just, and, a priori, anything that is bad or unjust must therefore be an aberration of religion" (Martin 2010: 3).[4] I clearly considered myself to have privileged access to what being a Protestant *really meant*, whilst also feeling I was above these prevalent identity politics: I might've been Northern Irish, but I apparently knew better.

Things became even more complicated when I moved to Edinburgh in 2004 to study for a degree in physics (go figure). On

---

4 Similar analysis is offered in Fitzgerald (2015a; 2015b), Martin (2010), Modood (2007), Swain (2016), and elsewhere.

the one hand, my accent was immediately and universally (though gently) mocked, which resulted in me (initially intentionally) all-but-losing my Northern Irish twang. (This can be temporarily rectified by the consumption of a few ales.) At the same time, due to "Chris" being a relatively common name, I quickly became known as "Irish Chris." My eyes were opened; I was able to embrace what I saw at that moment as the positive associations of an Irish identity (e.g., friendly, up for a laugh, strong, independent, etc.) whilst rejecting what I perceived to be the negative connotations of the added qualifier "Northern" (e.g., terrorism, sectarianism, closed-mindedness, etc.). I began to celebrate (that is, drink Guinness on) St Patrick's Day for the first time. I hung a Republic of Ireland flag in my hallway. To adopt Michel de Certeau's terminology, I began to *tactically* identify as Irish.

For de Certeau, *strategies* are utilized by the powerful, with the benefit of foresight and planning, while *tactics* tend to be more improvised and reactive, occurring on the battlefield as opposed to in the war room – think, for instance, of the difference between the position of manager and player, the training ground and the stadium. More specifically, as he put it, a strategy is the "calculation (or manipulation) of power relationships that becomes possible as soon as a subject with will and power [...] can be isolated" (1984: 35–6). It is a "prerogative of the powerful," demanding time, space, and panoptical vision (Woodhead 2012: 7). By contrast, "a tactic is a calculated action determined by the absence of a proper 'locus' that must be utilized in the space of the 'other,' as demarcated by the contextually relevant hegemonic power" (de Certeau 1984: 36–7). A census form, a passport, or a social scientist's apparatus might strategically place me in a fixed identity silo. However, just as Touna might stress a connection to Athens or Thessaloniki, all depending on circumstances, as I navigate the world, positioning myself and being positioned by others, different tactical identifications occur, each fabricating a particular authentic self to suit the specific context.

Might all of this make you think that I'm ashamed of being Northern Irish? Well, far from it (most of the time)! I hate hearing

"Great Britain" being used as if it's synonymous with the UK (it should be "Team UK" at the Olympics, not "Team GB," no?). I enjoyed supporting Northern Ireland and the Republic of Ireland in the recent Euro 2016 football tournament (and "anyone but England"),[5] and Ireland in any and every rugby union tournament screened in pub.[6] And I have been trying (fairly unsuccessfully) to reclaim my accent. However, something that I'm (now) ashamed of is the UK and what I perceive it to stand for. I'm well aware that this shame has developed over my time in Edinburgh, and been heavily influenced by my eventual shift to studying and working in the social sciences. After a significant "change of heart," I voted for Scotland to leave the UK in September 2014.[7] Unfortunately (for me) that did not happen. I also recently voted for the United Kingdom to remain in the European Union (EU).[8] Unfortunately (for us all) that did not happen. In these turbulent times, being (Northern) Irish gives me added kudos in a Scotland where I increasingly feel at home. It also means, pedantically, that I needn't be identified as British (I was not born on the island of Great Britain, after all), and this gives me increasing pleasure (conversely, I get increasingly annoyed when I exemplify a "typically British" trait). Of potentially more tangible benefit to me, my being born on the island of Ireland before 2004 (currently) entitles me to an Irish passport, and should hopefully imply the same for my wife, who was born in England, to a Northern

5 This is *nothing to do with* being anti-England, by the way, but with the resentment built up over a lifetime of living in the peripheral nations of the "United" Kingdom, and the mass media's assumption that we all therefore must care about how the hegemonic power performs in sporting events. (The fact that I felt the need to clarify this point speaks volumes here.)

6 Rugby is one of the few sports in which the island of Ireland fields a single team representing both nations.

7 Read my thoughts on this here: https://religionandmore.word-press.com/2014/09/10/why-i-am-voting-yes-to-scottish-independence/ (accessed July 18, 2016).

8 Read more about my rationale here: https://religionandmore.wordpress.com/2016/06/03/why-i-am-voting-to-remain-in-the-eu/ (accessed July 18, 2016).

Irish mother and an English father, and has lived almost all of her life in Scotland. Will this allow us to remain EU citizens? Well, we can hope so....

So, to return to my opening, at that farewell concert, although I cannot speak to whether "Anthem" from *Chess* should be "our" national anthem, it's certainly a good candidate for what I perceive to be my own idiosyncratic nation-of-one. And if my reflections above, combined with my pained attempt to utilize popular culture to position myself in some sort of enlightened post-nationality pan-optical space, tell you nothing else, they should demonstrate that not only is my (Northern) Irishness the product of a series of "operational acts of identification" (Bayart 2005: 92), but that it is ripe for analysis, as is this very essay.

# References

Bayart, Jean-François (2005). *The Illusion of Cultural Identity*. London: C. Hurst & Co. Publishers Ltd.

de Certeau, Michel (1984). *The Practice of Everyday Life*. Trans. Steven F. Rendall. Berkeley, CA: University of California Press.

Fitzgerald, Timothy (2015a). "Negative Liberty, Liberal Faith Postulates, and World Disorder." In Trevor Stack, Naomi Goldenberg, and Timothy Fitzgerald, eds., *Religion as a Category of Governance and Sovereignty*, 248–79. Leiden and Boston: Brill. https://doi.org/10.1163/9789004290594_012

Fitzgerald, Timothy (2015b). "Critical Religion and Critical Research on Religion: Religion and Politics as Modern Fictions." *Critical Research on Religion* 3(3): 303–19. https://doi.org/10.1177/2050303215613123

Hughes, Aaron W. (2015). *Islam and the Tyranny of Authenticity: An Inquiry into Disciplinary Apologetics and Self-Deception*. Sheffield: Equinox.

Liechty, Joseph and Cecelia Clegg (2000). *Moving beyond Sectarianism*. Blackrock, Co. Dublin: Columba Press.

Martin, Craig (2010). *Masking Hegemony: A Genealogy of Liberalism, Religion and the Private Sphere*. London: Routledge.

McGarry, John and Brendan O'Leary (1995). *Explaining Northern Ireland: Broken Images*. Oxford: Blackwell.

Modood, Tariq (2007). *Multiculturalism*. Oxford: Polity.

Mulholland, Marc (2003). *Northern Ireland: A Very Short Introduction.* Oxford: Oxford University Press. https://doi.org/10.1093/actrade/ 9780192801562.001.0001

Rice, Tim, Benny Andersson, and Bjorn Ulvaeus (1986). *Selections from Chess Songbook.* Milwaukee, WI: Hal Leonard.

Ruane, Joseph and Jennifer Todd (1996). *The Dynamics of Conflict in Northern Ireland: Power, Conflict and Emancipation.* Cambridge: Cambridge University Press. https://doi.org/10.1017/CBO9780511605598

Swain, Stacie A. (2016). "What's in a Name, a Name Rearranged? Part 1." *Practicum: Critical Theory, Religion, and Pedagogy.* April 20. http:// practicumreligionblog.blogspot.co.uk/2016/04/whats-in-name-name- rearranged-part-1.html (accessed June 14, 2016).

Woodhead, Linda (2012). "Strategic and Tactical Religion." Paper presented at the Sacred Practices of Everyday Life Conference, 1–15. Edinburgh: Religion and Society. Available at http://www.religionand-society.org.uk/attachments/files/1337692875_Woodhead-Tactical%20 Religion-Edinburgh%20May%202012.pdf (accessed June 20, 2016).

Christopher R. Cotter is founding editor and podcast co-host at the Religious Studies Project, and a PhD candidate at Lancaster University, UK. His research focuses upon the discourses on "religion," "non-religion," and "the secular," and the ensuing theoretical implications for Religious Studies. He is co-editor (with David G. Robertson) of *After World Religions: Reconstructing Religious Studies* (2016), and is Honorary Treasurer of the British Association for the Study of Religions.

# 7. Who Are You? I'm a Miser

## Steven W. Ramey

I tend to be careful about spending money. I almost always pack my lunch when I go to campus, and my family does not go out to eat or to the movies often. When we do eat in a restaurant, we order water to drink. Of course, we also drink mostly water at home, and we prefer to shop at thrift stores and used-book stores whenever we can. Such spending habits lead some people to see me as a tightwad or a miser like Ebenezer Scrooge. Perhaps even some in my household think that such a label is appropriate at times when they want something more. Naturally, given the negative connotations of those labels, I prefer the adjectives thrifty or sensible, even if everyone does not agree.

Any identification works this way. Even when people recognize the same general characteristic from the things a person does, tension can remain between self-selected labels and identities that other people ascribe to the person, as people associate various normative values and connotations with those labels. Labels that I select for myself reflect my interests in self-representation, and labels that others impose on me reflect their own assumptions and interests, interests that often include justifying their own choices as reasonable, particularly if they differ from mine.

Presuming agreement about those specific characteristics that lead to a contested label, like my spending practices that lead people to call me a miser or a thrifty spender, may also be inaccurate. Connecting particular actions to a personal characteristic depends on which practices a person notices. While I seldom eat out, I spend money on other things that I identify as important, but if someone else does not see those things as normal or important, then they can interpret my actions as being rather profligate, no matter what justifications I generate about my choices. So, in multiple ways, my spending habits and the ways I am labeled based on them depend on the perspective and emphases of the person generating the label more than something inherent within myself.

To make sense of the labels and the practices that generate them, I often construct a narrative that connects particular actions to a long-term, even inherited characteristic, making it appear intrinsic to my identity rather than a temporary or occasional choice. My origin tales for my propensity to frugality generate a notion of continuity with both my childhood and my family history. As a child, I remember learning the Boy Scout Law:

> A scout is Trustworthy, Loyal, Helpful, Friendly, Courteous, Kind, Obedient, Cheerful, Thrifty, Brave, Clean, and Reverent.

I can selectively highlight the ninth point – Thrifty – as a point of continuity with my upbringing, even as I ignore other issues in relation to Scouting that I may not fully accept now. In terms of inherent tendencies, I can also look back for generations to the thrifty nature of my grandparents, who chose not to spend much money even when they had it available. My parents maintained that philosophy of spending less and saving for the future which they learned from their parents. So, I come by my thriftiness honestly, as long as we ignore all the ways that I make choices about where to spend my money that are different than those of my grandparents or my parents.

This identification as thrifty and the ways that it can be contested, though, rely on a set of comparisons to friends and the larger society in which I live that we often treat as universal, even though these comparisons are clearly context-dependent. When I have visited India, for example, most of the people whom I met did not call me thrifty when I spent $15 a night for an air-conditioned room in a guest house or $1.50 for a Domino's pizza. While those prices and choices sound thrifty in the context of the United States middle class, as many hotels and restaurants in India can be much more expensive, let alone those in the United States, such choices do not fit with the spending practices of many in India who work and live in similar, professional, middle-class settings. So, beyond the selectivity involved in focusing on particular actions (and ignoring others), applying labels with positive or negative connotations, and developing a narrative of continuity to present a choice as a long-term or inherited trait, all of these designations have come from a stereotypical United States middle-class consumer context. What counts as thriftiness or miserliness depends on the community a person inhabits and the various choices and interests of whomever applies that label. As much as I identify as being thrifty (not miserly), that label, like any identification, is more about how I want to view myself and my relations to others than something inherent in the way I spend money (or don't).

Steven W. Ramey is a Professor in Religious Studies at the University of Alabama, where he also directs the Asian Studies Program. He has researched the contested constructions of identifications in contemporary India, which he addresses in his book *Hindu, Sufi, or Sikh* (2008). He has extended this analysis to reflect on issues in the academic and public discourse surrounding the category religion and issues of identifications in the United States and other contexts.

# 8.  Contesting Labels and the Study of Religion

## Anja Kirsch

Processes of labeling and storytelling are closely connected, as Steven Ramey points out in his essay. He begins with a personal statement about being thrifty, and specifies it with everyday examples. Then he seems to switch to another person's perspective on his spending habits, labeling himself a miser, like Ebenezer Scrooge. For those who grew up with Charles Dickens' *A Christmas Carol* or have seen one of the films, a picture of a grumpy, pinched-face, and cold-hearted old misanthrope comes to mind. The reference to a literary character immediately activates a cultural code for negatively connoted extreme frugality. It is "cured" in the novel by means of several ghosts who first make Scrooge glimpse his own lonely and loveless childhood, and then let him watch others celebrate Christmas. Scrooge finally develops empathy for his fellow human beings. But at other times and in a different context, Scrooge might have been considered differently by readers. To disapprove of Christmas and to be thrifty could be indicators of a good Puritan, who, in opposition to the story of Scrooge, is cured of reckless, worldly spending habits and whose increased wealth would then be read as evidence of his chosen status.

Ramey certainly has no ambition of being cured of his spending habits by supernatural agents, but he is no Puritan either. He explains how labels or classifications are based on different perspectives. As such, they are dependent on selective perception (for example, which practices do I notice and cite as evidence to conclude that someone else is either miserly or profligate?); comparison (in comparison to what or whom do I declare someone to be miserly or profligate?); and interpretation (what motivates me to translate an action, like a spending habit, into evidence of a personal characteristic?). While perception is largely culturally determined – e.g., spending $1.50 for a piece of pizza may be thrifty from the perspective of an American middle-class consumer, but it is certainly not thrifty from an Indian middle-class perspective – comparison is an attempt to justify a label as reasonable. Comparison is thus an integral part of the act of interpretation, one that relies on several strategies of sense-making.

One of these strategies is narrative. Every narrative starts with an activation of the reader's imagination, for instance by mentioning an everyday situation: "When we eat in a restaurant, we order water to drink." A concise sentence is sufficient to evoke a picture of the situation. Since we are all familiar with eating in a restaurant, we automatically relate "restaurant" to a chain of events, unnecessary to be told in further detail. But it is only in the context of the initial statement (I tend to be careful about spending money) that this situation seems to make a particular sense to us. References to literary characters may intensify this act of sense-making for they evoke even stronger pictures like that of Ebenezer Scrooge, Superman, or Jesus. Telling a story often invites a counter-story, an allegedly different perspective on an event. This change in perspective is a narrative strategy that serves to make one's own perspective even more plausible (for instance, telling oneself "My family considers me a miser, but that is because they want something from me"). Narratives of origin (e.g., how I became a miser or how frugality is related to my family history) are the most common way of explaining a particular behavior as an "inherited" characteristic. They are thus useful as identity practices. Of course these stories vary depending on who tells them (as well as where, when, and to whom!). As Steven Ramey points out, self-images and images of the other necessarily differ, leading to contested labels that reflect different interests.

As scholars we learn to question such labels, and we do so all the more if they seem obvious or self-evident. The study of religion examines processes of labeling; and our objects of study are, in a way, contested labels (such as classifying something as a ritual or as unorthodox). Furthermore, it is our job to examine labels (and their implications!) that are taken for granted by someone, such as naming something as a superstition, a world religion, or perhaps these practices as Hindu. Labeling processes do not only concern our objects of research but also ourselves, for instance when people sometimes speculate on features of our own biography by presuming they are linked to the research topics we choose to study. Take a labeling story that applies to me: I conducted a study of secular character education in the German Democratic Republic, the former socialist part of Germany (e.g., how the state tried, through a variety of its institutions, political strategies, and, not least, narrative practices to make what its leadership considered to be good or productive citizens); quite often learning this leads people to assume that I grew up in that country. It rarely occurs to them that I conducted my research because a systematic study on the meaning-making processes of socialism, carried out from the perspective of the study of religions, was lacking. My case is not exceptional. Similar suspicions might occur when scholars do research on such topics as women and Islam (with people sometimes concluding that she is researching this topic because she is a woman and/or married to a Muslim), Wiccan religion ("he must be neo-pagan…"), magic ("does she practice it herself?"), or contemporary atheism. I once witnessed a colleague who was, after his presentation on non-religion at a conference, asked by another colleague, quite out of the blue, if he was an atheist himself.

Do not misunderstand me: the question of how our research choices are driven by biographical connections is legitimate. Revealing our own guiding cognitive or social interests in doing our research is a matter of research ethics, so we teach our students to be critically self-aware and to make disclosures. So it is not my intent to doubt the validity of this practice. My impression, however, is that not all research topics provoke the question of biographical relatedness in equal measure. For instance, I have never heard someone speculate if a scholar of classical Roman or Greek religion is somehow Roman or Greek. Assuming biographical connections is apparently more plausible in the case of contemporary rather than historical research topics. At first glance, this seems to make sense.

But there is still no reason to assume that historical research is free of personal connections (after all, one could study ancient Greece in order to justify modern Greece, by assuming the two are somehow inherently linked).

Labeling is therefore one of our strategies to make sense of the world. But academia challenges us to query this habit and to transform it into methodology (the deliberate reflection on the tools we use). For scholars of religion, our most contested label is probably our key term: *religion*. To accept that "there is no data for religion" (Smith 1982: xi) does not mean that religion does not exist as an influential and successful category used by people to make sense of the world. People actually refer to religion all the time, to justify political viewpoints or to interpret their own experiences and actions or the actions of others. Of course, all these references are dependent on specific understandings of the label "religion." Consider the following everyday conversation:

> Person A: "I am not religious."
> Person B: "So you don't have any values, then?"
> Person A replies, maybe a bit indignantly: "Of course, I do!"
> Person B concludes: "So you *are* religious!"

Even though this may seem very simplistic, the identification of religion as a guarantee that someone has "values" and thus acts according to a code of behavior has an academic history. Think of Max Weber's observations about his visit to the United States, found in his essay "The Protestant Sects and the Spirit of Capitalism" (1905). Despite the official separation of church and state in the US, Weber witnessed people referring repeatedly to their church memberships in the context of being a trustworthy businessman or a solvent patient (Weber 2001: 128). In twentieth-century political analysis, the understanding of religion as a foundation of values has become a framework to explain the rise of political extremism in Europe. In *The Political Religions* (1938), Eric Voegelin explains the disastrous effects of the "estrangement from God" in modernity. It has led, he argues, to "false" religions such as fascism and National Socialism, which he understands to be the consequence of the lack of values in secularized modernity (Voegelin 2000: 23–4).

Academic research has significantly contributed to the identification of "religion" as a label for systems of values. It may also demonstrate the interactions of technical, or academic, definitions of this label with everyday understandings of the concept. As scholars, we are obligated to be aware of these reciprocal processes and to differentiate between everyday and academic understandings of religion. The latter is an analytic category that we use to name a subset of human actions or institutions. It is thus, as Jonathan Z. Smith has emphatically pointed out, "solely the creation of the scholar's study [...] created for [...] analytic purposes" (Smith 1982: xi). Nevertheless, by using the term to declare something or someone to *be religious*, we take part in generating the label religion, even though our label is a far more expansive and elastic term than its colloquial or everyday use may suggest. In principle, I see this as a benefit. To examine a label more closely can be a helpful strategy of demystification, revealing that concepts such as race, gender, or even religion are socially constructed and negotiated within the groups who use them to make their worlds meaningful in either this or that way. But we still need to consider that the subjects getting labeled may find our scholarly or outsider labels inappropriate since they also have a powerful social effect. Just as much as Steven Ramey does not want to be declared a tightwad or a miser, some people might not want to be labeled religious. For instance, when a colleague in Switzerland worked on a catalogue of local religious groups, the Freemasons protested against being included on his list. Today, the list is entitled *Religious Groups and Worldview Communities*, and the text describing this group mentions that the Masonic lodge does not see itself as a religious group but as "a worldview association." In this particular case, introducing another label seems to have solved the problem, but the general difficulty persists.

Labels are tricky. The study of religion, like all academic fields, does not only examine labels used by others or their processes of labeling the world; it also actively generates labels of its own and is thus involved in these processes too – we, as scholars, are making worlds of meaning as well. The best we can do when finding our-selves in this dilemma is to derive a consistent method and examine labeling processes systematically – all the more if they are our own. And this is what Steven Ramey does: he demonstrates how modes of labeling make a certain sense of himself plausible (though maybe not persuasive).

# References

Smith, Jonathan Z. (1982). *Imagining Religion: From Babylon to Jonestown.* Chicago: University of Chicago Press.

Voegelin, Eric (2000 [1938]). "The Political Religions." In Manfred Henningsen, ed., *Modernity without Restraint*, vol. 5, *The Collected Works of Eric Voegelin*, 19–73. Columbia and London: University of Missouri Press.

Weber, Max (2001 [1905]). "The Protestant Sects and the Spirit of Capitalism." In Stephen Kalberg, ed., *The Protestant Ethic and the Spirit of Capitalism*, 127–47. Chicago and London: Fitzroy Dearborn Publishers.

Anja Kirsch is a post-doctoral researcher at the University of Basel, Switzerland, and the Research Coordinator of the PhD program in Religious Studies of the Universities of Basel and Zurich. She specializes in the nar-rative relation of religion and the secular. Her research interests include the aesthetics of the secular, narrative efficacy and plausibility in literary aesthetics, and the relation between religion and narrative in film/media.

# 9. Who Are You? I'm a Leg Crosser

**Russell T. McCutcheon**

On occasion when students are in my office, and I'm trying to draw their attention to the sometimes subtle ways in which we act ourselves into certain sorts of identities, I'll ask them to take a quick look at how we're both sitting. There's a good chance that I'm behind my desk, reclining a bit in my office chair, with my legs crossed in that way that some adults will sometimes sit: one knee over the other, lower legs almost parallel, seated over on one haunch. And there's an equally good chance that the student I'm talking to is not seated like this. And so drawing attention to how we're both sitting – something that we've each done quite unselfconsciously, I'm sure – gives us a chance to think through identity as an empirically observable thing, as something we persuade ourselves and others that we have, not by expressing it but, rather, by repeatedly acting ourselves into it.

I'm hardly the first to think this – performativity studies abound. But sitting with a student in my office, each looking at who sits how, can be a great (because so seemingly mundane, so everyday, and thus so uncurious) way into this approach – *especially* if we see the behavior as creating the conditions for identification rather than what I take to be the more conservative approach of seeing the behavior as merely being the outward projection of what we commonly presume to be an unseen, ahistorical, and thus nonempirical inner impulse.

To jump ahead, I try to work students to the conclusion that it's not that I sit like this now *because I'm an adult*; instead, it may be the case that I am judged by others, even judged by myself, *to be* an adult *because I sometimes sit like this*. For as that old saying goes (credited to Mark Twain but dating back much longer), "clothes make the man" – and if you take that verb seriously, then you start to get a sense for the counter-intuitive position I'm arguing here, and not just about clothes.

Because counter-factuals are sometimes good to think with (i.e., think of an alternative condition or different result in order to make what in fact did happen appear to be far more curious), I have very clear memories of *not* sitting like that, when I was much younger, much like the memories of not eating certain foods when I was a kid, foods I then despised but foods that, as an adult, I now relish – "I would've never eaten this as a kid," I find myself saying sometimes at dinner. (But because I eat it now, I guess I'm all grown up?) And back then I knew that men – well, certain sorts of men, businessmen, men in three-piece suits, men at meetings, sophisticated men being interviewed on TV, men who carried briefcases – sat with their legs crossed like that and that I, not yet being a man, not carrying a briefcase, would be judged an interloper, a pretender, if I tried to sit like that.

"Act your age," someone might have said, in a disciplining tone, if I were to have sat like that as a kid; apparently, we act ourselves into an age.

If I trust my memory – and I'm not sure how wise that is, to be honest – I also knew that my, shall we say, manliness might be in question if I sat like that – so not just some ill-defined, sense of "maturity" is tied to posture and pose, but all sorts of other identifications circulate around those tightly crossed legs, such as age, class, power, and, in the case of males sitting that way, sometimes sexuality and thus their status – even their physical safety! – in a group. (I say "sometimes" because there are men whose rugged masculinity would never be in question even if seated in what some see, in some instances, as a feminine pose – indicating that, like all signifiers, this one is no less slippery and complex.)

Also, let's be honest: it was difficult to do, getting the legs crossed like that, since certain parts I had just seemed to get in the way, making it a bit of a puzzle, at least to my young self, how guys even did that.

I sometimes see men, already over on the one haunch, push one leg up and over the other, to get them to lock into position. It's hardly natural; it takes effort.

Looking back, it took me years of that very effort to feel legitimate sitting like a banker, an executive, or like a gentleman – training to emulate the figures around me who were modeling legitimacy for me, before I felt like I could own the posture and the social implications that came with it. I recall my mother buying me a briefcase when I first got into grad school – a black one with combination locks and everything, like James Bond might casually toss on the bed of a hotel room when checking-in to some exotic locale, careful when dialing the combination lock so as not to trip the booby trap contained inside. But I felt sort of silly carrying it around, like I was *playing at* being an adult. A backpack would do, I decided. It's what all the cool grad students were carrying (only one strap nonchalantly slung on one shoulder though, right? Both straps made it look like you were a little too earnest, maybe the kind of person who tucked your sweater inside your pants). Sitting like a banker was much the same.

But, for some reason, now it comes naturally. Correction: as if it is natural.

For, despite still feeling eighteen in many ways, I'm now fifty-five. At least as compared to my earlier self, unsure of the new selves it was slowly (inevitably?) becoming, a considerable amount of water has passed under the bridge, changing the bridge and the banks as it flowed; so while I've never quite grown into the sleek legitimacy of a black attaché case (preferring the casual, rustic legitimacy of a weathered leather book bag that I gave my wife as a graduation present, long ago), I now find myself sitting, one leg tightly draped over the knee of the other, without even thinking about it. While I can certainly still lean forward and throw my knees out wide while perching my elbows on them (communicating sincerity or eagerness, perhaps – "Do tell me more…"), maybe lean back and stretch my legs out straight with my ankles crossed, hands clasped behind my head and elbows out wide (telling the world how casual and, quite literally, laid-back I am, perhaps?), or sometimes cross my legs with one ankle atop a knee, so that my legs are at about 90 degrees to each other (formal, but not too formal, like wearing a tuxedo t-shirt), there's a pretty good chance that if I look at how my body has ended up being situated in space, I'm seated in a way I never felt confident enough to chance long ago.

All of which is to say that, in commenting on how I sometimes sit, I've just told you a great deal about my self now. For I've disclosed that I'm male (saying I "just sit" this or that way, without thinking, told you as much – male privilege, perhaps?) since most of the women whom I know easily recall, if asked, being taught how to "sit like a lady," usually around adolescence and thus puberty. But I've also told you that I grew up in a homophobic culture (thus my memory of an awareness, already at an early age, of those insecure concerns for how my posture might threaten my status and others' perceptions of me). So, too, I've made evident that I'm now a certain sort of professional, with a certain sort of cultural capital, who occupies a certain class position ("we" are the sort of people, after all, who call those with whom we work "colleagues," and so we can sit like that in meetings, discussing big ideas of big consequence). And you know that I'm a certain sort of age (an age different from those students coming by my office, many of whom just seem to flop into a chair to talk, sitting in a way likely rather different from how they will in just a few short years, when they're working somewhere – no longer dressed in t-shirts and flip-flops).

So who am I? I'm a middle-aged professor who sometimes sits in a certain way, and, every now and then, I try to use it, like a lot of other mundane things at his fingertips, as an example to make taken-for-granted situations a little more curious, that's who. But then again, just looking at me seated there might have already told you that.

Russell T. McCutcheon is Professor and Chair of the Department of Religious Studies at the University of Alabama. He has published widely on the study of religion's history and the politics of classification – specifically the socio-political uses of the taxon "religion" (whether employed as a folk or technical term).

# 10. Who Am I? Merely a Player

## Candace Mixon

I have a bit of trouble sitting – in some cases, I have trouble sitting still (what my partner calls my hummingbird heart), and in other cases, my feet don't quite touch the ground when I sit on many chairs. Most office chairs, library chairs, and even bar stools seem to have been made for the tall male bankers of yore that Russell McCutcheon has discussed. I can pretend to be taller – wear heels, but not too often or too high (must negotiate my sexuality at all times), look for a lever to raise or lower the seat – but regardless, seats are not often made for me. It is not only seats, but spaces too. Recent studies have shown that the frigid temperature of many office buildings was set to accommodate the temperaments of the male bankers donning three-piece suits. They dress for winter in the summer, while women still bring coats and blankets to work and to libraries to cover the bare shoulders of a summertime sheath (Belluck 2015). Working in places that are quite literally not cut out for you is the task not only of a female scholar in academia, but also the task of any woman graduate student. So we grin and bear it, and surprisingly few of us realize that all the world is a stage and we must play the part we have signed up for (or been cast in, depending on how you see it).

In the previous essay, McCutcheon wrote that he might be labeled a pretender if he tried to sit in a certain way, or carry a certain bag before his due time (is it 30? is it an MA? is it a PhD?). I argue here that the act of pretending is mostly all that we do, and as such, *we train to be better pretenders*. In order to pretend, one must have a goal: an image or ideal that one strives for, that one strives to be or effect in that moment. When I was five, I played pretend by

imagining my ample, rural, overgrown yard was actually a magnif-
icent garden off *Lifestyles of the Rich and Famous*.[1] I was neither
rich nor famous at five (and still am not!), but I watched a TV show
and sought to enact the behavior of one who was on the show. Pierre
Bourdieu in his short book, *On Television*, tells us, "The political
dangers inherent in the originary use of television have to do with
the fact that images have the peculiar capacity to produce what literary critics call a reality effect. They show things and make people
believe in what they show" (Bourdieu 1996: 21). When I was eighteen, I moved for the first time to a large metropolitan area for college in Nashville, and I needed to pretend not only that I belonged
in the playground of the kids who had literally grown up in their
own lifestyles of the rich and famous, but that I could also act natural within this urban environment. In these cases, and many others
happening almost every hour of the day (for example, this morning,
while walking my dog in Amsterdam, I pretended to speak Dutch
when another dog-owner greeted me, mostly because it was early
and I preferred to not have to engage in small talk as I would have
to if we switched to English), pretending is not some cover up of a
true identity in exchange for one that it is false or contrived. *It is my
identity itself* – a series of responses and actions that help me (and all
of us) get through both daily life and career. Pretending is not only
a step to get somewhere else (McCutcheon writes of his "training to
emulate the figures around me who were modeling legitimacy for
me"), but also the very act of identity-making itself.

If identity is not an eruption of the inner trait that becomes apparent and expressed in the world, as the introduction to this volume
argues, following Jean-François Bayart, then we are looking for
the "situationally-specific techniques for fabricating the impression
of authenticity, autonomy, and primordiality." In this case it is the
power to pretend that might be the most important power we have.
To pretend is to see that there is a goal, and to appear to have reached

---

1 This was a television show that ran from 1984 to 1995. The show
is utterly obsolete now, since only one show today could not suffice as a
venue for the excesses that seek display on television and social media.

that goal. The most obvious quip here is, "Fake it till you make it." However, I think to call it faking belittles the creativity and earnest work that comes through pretending.

Over my years as a graduate student, I have spent countless hours in libraries and archives or on Google, searching for this or that term, seeking out a connection between two ideas, or tracking down the smallest detail to complete a footnote. What I have learned in these latter days of my doctoral research is that (and this seems obvious only because we are told as doctoral students this is indeed our very job) I am the only one who knows the story I am writing, and the only one who can do it. In order to create knowledge (to bring to the fore a concept no one has discovered before, add something new to the academy, or reveal what has been in the shadows), which is the very goal of the dissertation, I perform the act of assertion and pretend to be the master. Jonathan Z. Smith has offered what is hopefully now for many the familiar advice: "For the self-conscious student of religion, no datum possesses intrinsic interest. It is of value only insofar as it can serve as exempli gratia of some fundamental issue in the imagination of religion. The student of religion must be able to articulate clearly why 'this' rather than 'that' was chosen as an exemplum. His primary skill is concentrated in this choice" (1982: xi). If I take seriously these words, then I pretend that this is the story I have to tell, in my grant applications, in my dissertation proposal, even while I am writing, until the writing is done (if it is ever!). I have also been instructed to persuade – to convince you, my reader, that the story I have assembled is real. This means the story I have told is plausible, the connections truly present, and that I have demonstrated this effectively. If I convince you, I have made it. I have faked it till I made it, and once I made it (that is, passed a defense, etc.), *it is true*.

In Saba Mahmood's highly influential book, *Politics of Piety*, she describes and theorizes her extended time spent with the women of a mosque movement in Cairo, Egypt. She argues against a liberal form of agency that only sees feminism through the lens of resistance to or emancipation from the norm of patriarchal power structures. To break out of this binary of oppression and resistance, she engages in a critical examination of agency to examine what she terms "ethical pedagogy." Ethical pedagogy is thus the means by which these women seek cumulative piety, or advancement in their spiritual progress through the means of their own learning structures and methods. Therefore, the women she studies are not passive acceptors of the system of Islamic learning around them, but they instead find ways to make space within and in spite of this system, through education and performance. Ethics in this case is a means of power by which individual actors condition themselves into being appropriately pious members of society. Whether it be reciting the Qur'an when you aren't impassioned to do so, or wearing a certain mode of pious dress, the practitioners see the acts of religious identity-making as having profound impact on the inner state of piety.

In the Cairo discussed above, Mahmood argues that the women strive towards the aggregation of morality through their practices of various pious acts. Put otherwise, Judith Butler has stated it is the "iterability of performativity that is a theory of agency" (1999: xxiv); thus, by continuously acting, one makes the self. By training the body through outward performances and religious education, these women may be *fabricating identities* with the goal of one day being fully aligned with this particular practice of faith.

As an example of "faking it till you make it," the situation above could fit the bill. In many cases of religious practice, acts such as the ones described above (e.g., dressing a certain way) are privileged as sacred, shielded from the language of faking or pretending, and instead fit in the descriptive space of authenticity and purity. In profane space, however, struggling with acceptance, accusations of faker and imposter syndrome, and pretending to have achieved what is still in progress is a part of daily life. In the act of identity-formation, pretending can and does occur everywhere, even in sacred spaces.

Heading back to who I am, I'll say it again: I am a player, and for now, graduate school is my stage. Each year in the month of May, when graduation ceremonies are happening, happiness exudes in the social media posts of many of my friends, who tend to be academics or those who have at least reached a Bachelor's degree. A Master's degree earned, a dissertation defended, more letters added to the name. Celebrations at every step! However, it is not only my friends earning advanced professional degrees, but now also the friends with children, celebrating the kindergarten graduation, the sixth grade graduation, the seventh (Billy Madison's formidable achievements and enviable parties also come to mind). Success at every turn perpetuates an incessant nudge to move up. With the constant presence of others' successes, I too must appear strong, accomplished.

I have tended to shy away from too many public announcements of my own successes; however, I assure you it is not out of my extreme humility or disavowal of public praise. Quite the opposite. Instead, I often (but not always) eschew the public announcements of my successes because the success usually means I am still in route to something else. When I earned my Master's degree, I didn't think twice about skipping graduation (after all, it was far away and there wasn't a distinct "cohort" with whom I clearly identified) since I was already two months into my doctoral program when my degree came in the mail. It seemed like a non-issue. I had performed the task in order to get to the next step, and the next step was already in progress by the time I was acknowledged.

As I step forward and keep moving along, I hold my head up confidently as I go, hoping not to trip over myself looking for the cue cards. Behind me though, there is a shadow. As I move towards the end of this graduate school act, I appear put together. I have been successful in earning many grants and fellowships to support my research, and I have a reputation as one who tirelessly pursues funding and opportunity. But this casts a shadow behind me as I share my secrets and tips with my own doctoral cohort and those that follow in my program, even sharing my knowledge publicly in graduate student sessions at the American Academy of Religion. However, the only secrets I have to share are the cues I get along the way that make my performance look natural, as if I've never forgotten my lines, or it is my hundredth time on stage. Right now, however, the air is too cool and the chair is not that comfortable, but the show must go on.

# References

Belluck, Pam (2015). "Chilly at work? Office formula was devised for men."
    *The New York Times*, August 3. http://www.nytimes.com/2015/08/04/
    science/chilly-at-work-a-decades-old-formula-may-be-to-blame.html
    (accessed July 26, 2016).
Bourdieu, Pierre (1996). *On Television*. Trans. Priscilla Parkhurst Ferguson.
    New York: New Press.
Butler, Judith (1999). *Gender Trouble: Feminism and the Subversion of
    Identity*. New York: Routledge.
Mahmood, Saba (2004). *Politics of Piety: The Islamic Revival and the
    Feminist Subject*. Princeton, NJ: Princeton University Press.
Smith, Jonathan Z. (1982). *Imagining Religion: From Babylon to Jonestown*.
    Chicago: University of Chicago Press.

Candace Mixon is a PhD candidate in Religious Studies, with a focus on Islamic Studies, at the University of North Carolina at Chapel Hill. Her dissertation is on material artifacts of devotion to the family of the Prophet Muhammad in contemporary Iran. She is especially interested in how Shi'ite devotion is gendered, materialized, and ritualized.

# 11. Who Are You? I'm a Feminist

## Leslie Dorrough Smith

I received a touching note from one of my graduating seniors this past week, who said, among other things, that I taught her that she did not have to fear calling herself a feminist. Every time I have a student tell me this, I consider the irony of my own response when, as an undergraduate, one of my Religious Studies professors handed me a photocopied article entitled "Jesus Was a Feminist."[1] The author, Leonard Swidler, forwards the basic thesis (now considered quite tame in many circles) that the Bible depicts Jesus as a person who cared about gender equity in a society that did not. I freely admit that, at the time, I had no academic exposure to gender theory, and even though I was acutely aware of sexism, I had never heard the term "feminist" used in a positive light. In short, I remember being appalled at the article.

Fast-forward a couple of decades: I now direct a Women's and Gender Studies program at the university where I teach, and I am a person who is (perhaps obviously) proud to call herself a feminist. Like many others, I understand feminism as the identification, interrogation, and dismantling of various forms of identity-based oppressions, including the well-known arenas of sex, gender, and sexual orientation. Feminist studies is not, however, limited just to sex and gender issues, but is a field also highly interested in the ways that those realms intersect with race, class, age, ability, and many other forms of social identity.

---

1 Leonard Swidler, "Jesus Was a Feminist," http://www.godswordto-women.org/feminist.htm. First published in *Catholic World*, 1971 (accessed January 31, 2016). Swidler went on to publish a book by the same name.

In light of this definition, I share the frustration of others when I hear feminism equated with hatred, or when some people attempt to render it irrelevant by claiming that, as a society, we have resolved most major forms of bias. While I would love nothing more than for that sort of irrelevancy to be true, the improvements that have been made on the gender front (to name just one example) have been met with equally formidable setbacks and stagnations that make gender and other forms of social inequity very real, indeed.

However, rather than go down that familiar road where I tell you about how awful it is that many misunderstand what feminism is, my interest in discussing the term goes back to how social groups create the strategies behind naming. Craig Martin recently wrote about the rhetorical power of an oversimplified (yet effective) definition of feminism, thinking through its strategic value rather than accuracy of content.[2] Martin describes how simply describing feminism as "gender equity" may take some of the punch out of what could otherwise be (and, in the past, has been) a more radical social movement, considering the fact that many people today don't find the proposition of gender equity very controversial. Regardless, he notes, what might be understood as the "watering down" of feminism might also lend it rhetorical strength insomuch as oversimplifying the definition might cause more people to think of themselves as feminists and thus increase their overall sympathy with the movement. In light of Martin's argument, I would like to further consider the possible identity dynamics involved when one agrees with the major tenets behind feminism but is hesitant to claim the name.

While there have been organized movements of progressives who have rejected the term "feminism" for a variety of reasons, I suspect that most who admire feminist concepts but reject the title do so because of a very popular idea that feminism is such a bad, divisive, or otherwise nasty thing that no likeable person would willfully adopt it. This is certainly one of the most frequent ways

---

2  See Craig Martin, "Reorganizing Sympathies." Culture on the Edge Blog, http://edge.ua.edu/craig-martin/reorganizing-sympathies/. Published November 7, 2013 (accessed January 30, 2016).

that I find myself discussing the term, for almost all of the students who take my gender and feminist theory classes find a lot of personal resonance with feminist ideals, but most report having to put up with a fair bit of harassment from family and friends for taking a course related to feminism in the first place.

But what is important to point out is that the negative connotations given to the term "feminism" are no historical accident. Every major feminist movement that has taken place in the US has been met by staunch opposition, with each new opponent claiming that feminism will annihilate everything good about American culture. Of course, the nation appears to have survived these shifts, which have included campaigns to give women and other minority groups voting and basic civil rights, educational access, equal wages for equal work, reproductive control, and most recently, equal marriage rights. Although a few of these items still remain controversial, the majority of Americans, when polled, find most of these items agreeable, and yet, again, comparatively few of them identify as feminists.

Much of the anti-feminist rhetoric that punctuates politics today is a recuperation of themes from the 1960s and '70s, when predominantly white, conservative Christian groups reacted negatively to a greater equalization of power relationships for women and racial minorities. My recent book on the group Concerned Women for America (CWA) provides an overview of the myriad ways in which CWA has engaged in decades of anti-feminist advocacy by claiming that working women, lesbians, and liberals, in general, are embodiments of a moral ineptness that will taint, and destroy, American culture (Smith 2014). Despite its longstanding trend of blaming feminism for most of America's problems, CWA began calling itself a "true" feminist organization several years ago to bolster its claim that traditional gender arrangements actually maximize female empowerment.

Many progressive voices have cried foul at CWA's changing self-representation on the matter of feminism, charging it with the height of hypocrisy. However, for those of us interested in the mechanics behind identity-building, I suspect that the lessons to be learned from these adoptions and refusals of the term "feminism" is that our self-identifiers often have less to do with our own beliefs and positions than they do with whether we will be read as socially valuable when (and if) we own the term. For CWA, rejecting but then later claiming feminism has been a part of a sophisticated move to render itself more powerful in different cultural circumstances when feminism has been either less or more (respectively) popular. To be clear, CWA's ideology hasn't radically changed; its term for what it calls its ideology has. And while my own decision to own the term "feminism" came about as my ignorance and fear about the term faded, it was only when I was introduced to the term as an acceptable (if not admirable) label that I had the courage to call myself a feminist. Again, I didn't experience a fundamental ideological change, but adopted a new term to describe it.

So when I say that "I am a feminist," I am not only making a statement about how I think that the world *should* operate, but I am also, on some level, acknowledging the specific way that it *currently* operates for me: at present, most of my major professional and personal relationships are not threatened by my adoption of the term; if anything, they are aided by it. I have enough privilege to be able to use it without much social resistance, and thus I use it consistently and openly in the hope that I will normalize it for others. While the term "feminism" is a veritable gold mine in discussions of identity politics, what I think this instance demonstrates is that the terms that we use to describe ourselves may often have far more to do with being perceived as normal than with being perceived as right.

# Reference

Smith, Leslie Dorrough (2014). *Righteous Rhetoric: Sex, Speech, and the Politics of Concerned Women for America*. New York: Oxford University Press. https://doi.org/10.1093/acprof:oso/9780199337507.001.0001

Leslie Dorrough Smith is Associate Professor of Religious Studies and Director of the Women's and Gender Studies program at Avila University. Her research focuses on the impact of religious rhetoric on attitudes and policy towards sex, gender, and reproduction in the United States. She is the author of *Righteous Rhetoric: Sex, Speech, and the Politics of Concerned Women for America* (2014).

# 12. Atheism and Its Consequences

## Ian Alexander Cuthbertson

For the last three years I have taught a large first-year undergraduate Introduction to Religious Studies course. Each year a few of my students ask me whether I am religious and, if so, which religion I follow. I imagine that students have two possible motives for asking this question: either they want to tease out possible bias in my teaching or else they want to know more about who I am as a person. But no matter their motives, the question always frustrates me. Throughout the course, I stress the importance of methodological agnosticism or the importance of bracketing one's own belief (or lack of belief) in the truth claims put forward by the various institutions and individuals who self-identify as "religious" that we study. I also stress that labels (e.g., Christian, Buddhist, etc.) always fail to capture the lived complexity of any individual's beliefs, half-beliefs, practices, or doubts. So the "what is your religion?" question frustrates me because my students ought to know that my particular religious affiliation (or lack thereof) should not affect my teaching and that even if I did confess to being Christian or Buddhist this would reveal very little about who I am – though it would give us an opportunity to investigate a moment of strategic identity formation.

But the question also frustrates me because I suspect many of my students already have an answer in mind when they ask me whether or not I'm religious. To give a typical example: during my office hours one spring a student casually asked me whether I was religious. Before I could answer she leaned forward and said, almost conspiratorially, "You're an atheist, aren't you?"

I like to pretend that I never answer the "what is your religion?" question because I want to turn the question into a teachable moment and make a point about the academic study of religion. But the truth is that I am afraid to answer it. The students are right. I am an atheist. But the prospect of openly inhabiting that label carries consequences and these consequences terrify me.

There are plenty of valid reasons to fear openly self-identifying as an atheist. Apostasy, or the abandonment of religious belief, remains illegal in nearly twenty countries around the world including Egypt, Iran, Afghanistan, Pakistan, Saudi Arabia, and Nigeria. Legal consequences for abandoning religion in these countries can be severe, ranging from fines to the death penalty. Although not all atheists have, strictly speaking, abandoned religious belief – some never had such beliefs to begin with – passively lacking a belief in god(s) is often conflated with actively denying the existence of god(s). Luckily, I happen to live in Canada where it is perfectly legal to deny the existence of god(s).

Yet apostasy is not the only crime with which an atheist can be charged. While only a few countries have apostasy laws, nearly a quarter of the world's countries have blasphemy laws. Such laws prohibit individuals from insulting, showing contempt for, or demonstrating a lack of reverence to a god or gods. Blasphemy laws are common in Europe and in the Americas as well: Greece, Italy, Germany, Poland, Ireland, Peru and Canada all have laws prohibiting blasphemy. While section 296 of Canada's criminal code states, "every one who publishes a blasphemous libel is guilty of an indictable offence and liable to imprisonment for a term not exceeding two years," blasphemers have also been punished with deportation on top of time spent in prison. Eugene Sterry, who became an atheist as a child, was found guilty of blasphemy after a one-day trial and was deported from the country sixty days later for, among other things, describing god's "frenzied megalomaniac boasting" (Patrick 2010). Does lacking any belief in god constitute a blasphemous libel? Surely doubting or denying the existence of god(s) must be worse than merely describing god in unflattering terms. Luckily, it is unlikely I will ever find out what constitutes blasphemy in Canada.

Eugene Sterry was tried and deported in 1927, and while Canada's blasphemy law remains "on the books" it has only been enforced five times since the criminal code was enacted and has not been enforced at all in the last sixty years.

Self-identifying as an atheist may have negative consequences even in countries where neither apostasy nor blasphemy are criminal offenses. In the United States, for instance, the social cost of self-identifying as an atheist can be high, especially for those who aspire to hold public office. The State Constitutions of Arkansas, Maryland, Mississippi, North Carolina, Tennessee, and Texas all prohibit atheists from holding governmental posts. As article 14, section 265 of Mississippi's constitution puts it, "no person who denies the existence of a Supreme Being shall hold any office in this state." Similarly, North Carolina's constitution disqualifies "any person who shall deny the being of Almighty God" along with persons convicted of treason or other felonies from holding office. Such constitutional prohibitions often depend on doubts concerning the reliability of atheist oaths of office – a doubt shared by the seventeenth-century philosopher, John Locke who argued, "promises, covenants, and oaths, which are the bonds of human society, can have no hold upon an atheist" (Locke 2002). But atheism and politics seem not to mix even when constitutional prohibitions are absent. Consider that although atheists are not constitutionally disqualified from becoming president, a 2016 PEW Research Center study indicates that Americans would rather elect a president who has smoked marijuana, is gay or lesbian, has had personal financial troubles, or has had extramarital affairs than a president who does not believe in god.[1]

While atheists may be deemed untrustworthy in America, they are also sometimes deemed offensive. Shannon Morgan learned this in 2014 when she requested a vanity license plate reading "8THEIST" from the New Jersey Motor Vehicle Commission. Her request was

---

1 "How Americans Feel About Religious Groups." www.pewforum. org. 2016. http://www.pewforum.org/2014/07/16/how-americans-feel-about-religious-groups/ (accessed June 1, 2016).

denied since, according to the commission, the proposed license plate carried "connotations offensive to good taste and decency."[2] In this way the title "atheist," like the title "feminist" (as explored by Dorrough Smith above), suffers from the very popular idea that atheism is "such a bad, divisive, or otherwise nasty thing that no likeable person would willfully adopt it." (In Canada, however, atheists receive less social disapprobation. Although the Canadian Charter of Rights and Freedoms [1982] begins with the statement "Whereas Canada is founded upon principles that recognize the supremacy of God..." my nonbelief in god[s] does not disqualify me from running for office and I have never yet been the victim of atheist discrimination.)

Atheists in the US and elsewhere have therefore come to realize that that the label atheist carries negative connotations: aside from being untrustworthy and indecent, atheists are also sometimes seen to be angry or militant. In part, these appraisals stem from the rise of so-called New Atheism and the publication of a number of books in the mid-2000s that loudly criticized religion, including Richard Dawkins' *The God Delusion* (2006); Christopher Hitchens' *God Is Not Great: How Religion Poisons Everything* (2007); Sam Harris' *The End of Faith: Religion, Terror, and the Future of Reason* (2004); and Daniel Dennett's *Breaking the Spell* (2006).

Yet even the New Atheists have also recently attempted to soften their public image. Richard Dawkins, inspired by what he calls feminist attempts to raise consciousness through gender-inclusive language (e.g., chairperson, not chairman) considers "the homosexual hijacking of the word 'gay'" to be a "triumph of consciousness-raising."[3] Recognizing that labels matter, Dawkins has suggested that atheists rebrand themselves as "Brights," noting that this label,

2 Elizabeth Landers, "Atheist Sues over New Jersey License Plate Refusal." CNN.com. 2014. http://www.cnn.com/2014/04/19/us/new-jersey-atheist-plates/ (accessed June 3, 2016).

3 Richard Dawkins, "The Future Looks Bright." https://www.theguardian.com/books/2003/jun/21/society.richarddawkins (accessed June 3, 2016).

like "gay," is more positive, warm, and cheerful. Yet New Atheists have also recognized that the opposite of bright (dim? dull?) has potentially negative connotations. So, in keeping with their desire to soften their image, they sometimes refer to individuals who believe in supernatural forces or god(s) as "Supers." Still, I suspect that calling myself a Bright would likely carry all the negative connotations of "atheist." Also, my fear of admitting that I am an atheist is only partially linked to the way this term might cast me as angry or militant in my disbelief.

I have sometimes self-identified as an atheist in order to resolve the confusion my two degrees in Religious Studies sometimes creates. For years I had to patiently explain to parents, friends, and strangers that I was not studying to become a priest or minister. Calling myself an atheist seemed like an easy remedy for this problem – until recently, that is. Gretta Vosper has been the minister at Toronto's West Hill United Church for nearly twenty years. Aside from being a minister in Canada's largest Protestant denomination, Vosper is also an atheist. As I write this, the United Church of Canada is reviewing one of its ministers for the first time in an attempt to decide whether an atheist like Vosper should be permitted to lead her congregation. Whatever its decision, the existence of an atheist minister problematizes my use of this label to indicate that I am not and never will be priest or pastor.

Another reason I consider myself an atheist is that I felt it clearly indicated that I do not believe in the existence of god(s) – again, until recently. Frank Schaeffer is an author, former evangelical leader, and an atheist. Schaeffer also believes in god. In his recent book *Why I am an Atheist Who Believes in God* (2014), Schaeffer reveals that he simultaneously believes and does not believe in god. As was the case with Vosper, Schaeffer's dual belief and disbelief problematizes my use of this label to indicate that I do not believe in the existence of god(s).

But shoes have also challenged my use of the label "atheist." The Berlin-based startup, Atheist Shoes, describes its shoes as "outspoken" and as a "powerful yet understated way for heathens to be more open about their godlessness."[4] Atheist Shoes made headlines recently when they reported that shipments to the United States branded with the word "atheist" were more likely to be lost or remain undelivered than identical shipments without the atheist branding. While this may speak to atheist discrimination in the US, it also demonstrates how labels (and controversy) are important not only for individuals but for businesses too. In other words, atheism sells.

But my fear of claiming the label "atheist" is not a result of possible legal reprisals, potential social costs, worries that I will appear aggressive or arrogant, or concerns that I may be mistaken for a shoe. I am afraid to call myself an atheist because I can never be sure what kinds of meanings this term will form in the minds of others. The label atheist (like any label) is not one that I control. It is powerful and fluid and this power and fluidity make me nervous.

But my reluctance to lay claim to the atheist label might in fact be selfish. Again, Dorrough Smith begins her reflection on feminism with the story of a young student who overcame her fear of inhabiting the label "feminist" after taking one of her courses. This made me wonder about my interactions with my students. Maybe, when that student leaned forward and said, "You're an atheist aren't you?" she was struggling with her own self-identification. Maybe she too wanted someone to show her that inhabiting this label is acceptable, whatever it might mean for her.

While labels can never capture the complexity of an individual's beliefs, thoughts, fears, or desires, they are important for the articulation of identities. Identities are always strategic constructions and the labels we use to articulate these identities entail consequences. But my own strategic refusal to self-identify entails consequences too. In the same way that I cannot control the implications of self-identifying as an atheist, I also cannot control the implications of refusing to self-identify as one either. Sometimes it is appropriate and necessary to problematize identities and labels. But again, as

4 "Ich Bin Atheist." http://www.atheistberlin.com/atheist (accessed June 4, 2016).

Dorrough Smith has shown, it is also sometimes appropriate and necessary to inhabit a particular self-identification and to share this with others. Refusing to self-identify can foreclose meaningful conversations and while I may not believe in god(s), I do believe in the value and importance of meaningful conversation.

## References

Locke, John (2002 [1869]). "A Letter Concerning Toleration." In Tom E. Crawford, ed., *The Second Treatise of Government and a Letter Concerning Toleration*. Devon: Dover Thrift Editions.

Patrick, Jeremy (2010). "Canadian Blasphemy Law in Context: Press, Legislative, and Public Reactions." *Annual Survey of International & Comparative Law* 16(1): 129–63.

Ian Alexander Cuthbertson received his PhD in Cultural Studies in 2016, exploring how dominant conceptualizations of modernity as secular and disenchanted render beliefs and practices associated with magical objects invisible to contemporary scholarship. Currently, Ian is interested in the ways non-religious individuals conceptualize both their non-religious identities and the place of religion in the contemporary Canadian context.

# 13. Who Are You? I'm a Vegetarian

## Steven W. Ramey

When I identify as a vegetarian, I occasionally face questions such as "What do you eat?" or "How can you give up bacon?" Those questions and related experiences reflect the dominance of meat within contemporary American food cultures generally. Occasionally, someone will ask a more knowledgable question, clarifying whether I am vegan or eat eggs, dairy, and even seafood. In some parts of Asia, those who identify as vegetarian typically do not hear as many questions because vegetarian cuisine, and often a particular type of vegetarianism, is common and has been for a long time.

Yet, even across Asia with long histories of vegetarian cuisine in many places, what a person means when they identify as a vegetarian can vary, as the label cloaks significant diversity. Some vegetarians consider seafood to be acceptable (and they have a separate subgroup, pescatarians). Some vegetarians do not want to eat anything, such as honey or animal-derived gelatin, that has required the death of a sentient creature to produce. Others refrain from eating meat but are more lenient on other animal-derived foods, such as milk and eggs, or they do not worry about small additives like fish sauce in otherwise vegetarian dishes, especially when they do not prepare food themselves.

Those are only a few of the differences among the people grouped together as vegetarians. Motivations also can be extremely varied. Some refrain from consuming meat because they do not like its taste or texture; for others it is a sacrifice that they take on out of an ethical concern for the treatment of animals and the inherent violence in meat production or an environmental concern about the greater range of resources required to produce meat than vegetarian options. For some, being vegetarian correlates with their identification as an "animal lover," while others consider vegetarianism to be a requirement to remain pure from a pollution that they associate with meat consumption based on particular community standards that we might identify as religious. And these different motivations overlap, as many who refrain from eating meet express different combinations of motivations that reinforce each other.

So, my identification does not delineate clearly what I choose to eat and what I avoid, or the reasons behind it. In fact, what counts as "meat" that a vegetarian avoids not only varies from person to person but also can shift over the course of a person's time identifying as a vegetarian. What I am willing to eat has certainly shifted over the years that I have identified as a vegetarian.

The identification also provides a weak basis for uniting a group. Imagine organizing a dinner party for a group of vegetarians. Arranging the meal, as a good host, in a way that satisfies everyone in the group, can be virtually impossible. If you only serve vegan fare, some who enjoy eggs and dairy might be disappointed. Serving selections from the different general understandings of vegetarianism might make some uncomfortable if dishes adhering to their more limited diet could be cross-contaminated with less-restrictive vegetarian dishes on the buffet. Some vegetarians have other food restrictions, whether by preference, allergy, or diet. Despite stereotypes, you cannot assume that all vegetarians like avocado and sprouts on their sandwich. Many vegetarians will be polite and understanding of these challenges; they have to be in a society in which their diet is not dominant, yet the complications illustrate well how vegetarians are not a unified group.

Beyond having many different reasons for and understandings of vegetarian practices, those who identify as vegetarians do not hold the same interests, making the dinner party host's plans for safe topics for conversation similarly complicated. The socio-economic and political commitments of vegetarians are not uniform, just as the motivations for being vegetarian are varied, despite stereotypes of young liberal elites.

So, why do I employ this label that provides limited clarity? I often alert others that I am a vegetarian when I receive an invitation to eat with them. But the practical interest in having something that I consider to be acceptable for me to eat is only part of my strategic identification. Because food is an important component of our social interactions, I want to make vegetarian choices more widely accepted and less isolating in this society in order to make the choice easier for myself and others to make. In a sense, I want to promote pride in being vegetarian and acceptance and accommodation from others for vegetarians.

When analyzing the dynamics of identification, it is intriguing to me what labels do and do not tell us. Having used several hundred words to discuss my identification as a vegetarian, how much do you really know about who I am, or even what I eat and why? So, even as I answer the question "Who are you?" my answer tells you a limited amount about me while serving my purposes to accomplish something beyond identifying myself.

Steven W. Ramey is a Professor in Religious Studies at the University of Alabama, where he also directs the Asian Studies Program. He has researched the contested constructions of identifications in contemporary India, which he addresses in his book *Hindu, Sufi, or Sikh* (2008). He has extended this analysis to reflect on issues in the academic and public discourse surrounding the category religion and issues of identifications in the United States and other contexts.

# 14. You Are What You Eat

## Sarah E. Dees

"You are what you eat." This popular phrase suggests that the food we ingest reflects on us in some material or immaterial way. Parents might say it to their children as a warning against feasting on sweets. Fitness enthusiasts might use the phrase as a form of inspiration along the path to their body-sculpting goals. Certainly, what we eat can affect our bodies and how we feel on both a short-term and long-term basis. We can also interpret the phrase as having an ethical or moral connotation. Within broader conversations of consumerism or agribusiness, the phrase suggests that beyond the nutrients that we are putting into our bodies, the types of foods that we consume – fast foods, slow foods, local foods, organic foods – implicate us in our support of larger types of farming, labor, and environmental practices. On a more nuanced level, then, this phrase seems to imply that what a person eats reflects some essential aspect of his or her identity.

A discussion of food and eating is important within the conversations scholars of religion have about individual and group identity. This topic raises a number of interesting questions about the nature of religious identity. What factors determine what we eat? What role does personal choice of diet have in determining identity? What are the limits of associating identity with personal choices? Where are the intersections between individual decision-making and greater systems of identifying, labeling, and managing individual and communal food practices?

In his essay, Steven Ramey argues that the category of "vegetarian" is not as useful as it might seem as a marker of identity. He points out that there are many different types of vegetarians – some that choose to eat eggs or dairy products and others that avoid all forms of animal products. Further, vegetarians cite numerous reasons for not eating meat, from matters of taste to ethical reasons. If we find the larger category of "vegetarian" to be ultimately unsatisfying, we might try to break it down even further, which offers some additional clarity into specific types of vegetarian diets and the purposes behind these. We could classify all of the different types of diets that restrict meat consumption: ovo-lacto-vegetarian, lacto-vegetarian, ovo-vegetarian, pollotarian, pescatarian, flexitarian, vegan, freegan. We could also consider different rationales behind choosing this type of diet: taste, nutritional, economic, religious, or ethical reasons. Yet ultimately, we still encounter difficulties when trying to separate individuals into these groups. The subcategories offer clarity on one level, but still obscure other cultural or social particularities. As Ramey suggests, the category of vegetarian ultimately "provides a weak basis for uniting a group" due to the many other differences vegetarians might have. If this is the case, what use might this and related categories offer for scholars of religion?

A discussion of food and eating is relevant within the field of religious studies and even cultural studies more broadly. Food studies is a growing subfield within anthropology, within which scholars examine all aspects of food production and consumption. Narrowing our perspective even further to the academic study of religion, food is an important topic. "Religious literacy," or the basic familiarity with aspects of well-known religious traditions, often touches on food practices. Practitioners of some religions may abstain from particular types of food at all times or on particular days. During the period of Lent, for example, some Christians abstain from eating food on Fridays. Muslims fast during the month of Ramadan. Adherents of numerous religious traditions – Jews, Christians, Muslims, Hindus, Jains – abstain from eating particular types of meat or combinations of food. Many religious laws or texts offer guidance on how to properly prepare dishes for human consumption or as offerings to deities. For adherents of nearly all organized religions, eating plays a key role in important ritual practices.

Of course, for those interested in more than a cursory understanding of religion, including the way the concept of religion operates in culture, analyses of food practices can be useful. Thinking closely about food can illuminate our understanding of how society and culture are constituted, including the development and continuation of communal beliefs and practices, and the ways in which these practices are adapted and reformed over time. Over generations, communal practices change as individuals with knowledge about their communities' past practices respond to new contexts and situations. As chapters in this volume indicate, the features that some groups consider to be a key part of their identity developed in particular historical contexts. What do we make of the role food plays in determining group identity? It is interesting to consider how and why adherents of groups have continued some food practices while others disregarded those aspects of religious law pertaining to food. Thinking about food can also help us understand tensions between larger group expectations and individual practices challenging those expectations.

The question of food and diet can also help us to think through the relationship that different religious communities identify between what they perceive to be "secular" and "religious" institutions, practices, and spaces. This is not, of course, to assume that there are essentially different secular or religious spaces, but to urge us to examine how individuals and communities make these distinctions for themselves. Some aspects to consider include the controversy about the sacrifice of chickens among Santerían communities in Florida (the Afro-Caribbean tradition that blends Roman Catholic and West African influences), despite the longstanding practice in the United States of ritually consuming turkeys during the nationally-recognized Thanksgiving holiday. What practices are considered ethical (or even just normal) while other, similar practices are considered immoral or impure? Pursuing this line of inquiry leads us to fascinating cultural moments and movements related to everything from popular culture to structural social inequalities in the United States and around the globe, from Christian American dieting fads to questions about social status and dietary practices in India.

Beyond the matter of personal taste, it is important to consider larger factors that shape what people eat. Ramey's analysis focuses on a context in which individuals and communities engage in self-determined dietary practices. In consumer societies, we assume that people *choose for themselves* what to eat from a variety of available options. One can therefore *decide* to become a vegetarian, or eat animals that have been raised ethically, or go on a paleo diet, or source food from within a thirty-mile radius, or eat only processed food. Vegetarianism may seem like one healthy enough *choice* among many (although a cheese-pizza-and-potato-chips version of vegetarianism is also an option for the less health-conscious). Students new to the study of religion also sometimes think of religion itself in terms of *personal choices*. Perhaps influenced by the consumer model of religion that permeates popular society, some of my students have initially suggested that people are born with some aspects of their identities, such as ethnicity, *but that religion is something that individuals can choose*.

However, neither dietary practices nor religious traditions are always about choice. For adherents of some religions, their participation involves not "freedom" but the surrender of personal choice. Religious traditions often dictate how, when, where, and what one might eat. Some religious ascetics beg for their food, and only eat what their benefactors give them. Texts that are significant for members of different traditions often touch on food practices. Of course, there is not one "Hindu" way to eat, nor one "Christian" way to eat – ultimately, groups of adherents, and not simply individuals, determine how to interpret significant texts. Examining the ideas that different members within those communities have about how to interpret texts' discussions of food practices can therefore tell us something about what they value, or how they respond to new innovations. We can learn about different roles that community members might have based on other aspects of their identities – such as gender or age – as well as relationships among members of specific communities and between these individuals and members of other groups. In other words, studying food practices can be a starting point to learn about other features of groups and societies rather than a final measure of group identity.

When looking at these communities, we must also consider larger factors that play some sort of a role in determining individuals' identities. Many individuals and communities determine their food practices for reasons not ethical but practical, including cost, convenience, and availability. Vegetarianism itself might be a necessary choice (and thus is it really best understood as a choice?) if meat prices are too expensive. (Poor people, one might say, don't *choose* to not buy a yacht – the choice has been made for them by the yacht's cost.) During times of major economic pressure in the United States, such as the Great Depression or the Second World War, many families were not able to purchase meat. Economic, political, and social forces therefore resulted in the development of recipes that used expensive or rationed food items sparingly and relied on home-grown food. Popular sentiment in this era celebrated the virtues of simple recipes (For example, I am quite fond of a WWII-era vegan chocolate cake.) This points to the ways in which broader forces – economic, social, political – limit the extent to which individuals and collectives can actually make choices about the food that they produce and consume.

To further understand the constraints on individuals' or groups' food consumption, scholars of religion should also think about larger mechanisms that constrain culture and identity, including the ways in which governments have regulated both religious practices and food practices. One historical example illuminates each of these forms of regulation: the US government's management of the bison population in the late-nineteenth century. Seeking to contain and control Plains Native American nations whose lands they sought, agents of the US government called on marksmen to train their rifles on American bison, animals that had long been important to Lakota and other groups. As a result, in the last decade of the nineteenth century, the bison neared extinction in America. Federal Indian agents intended to restrict Lakotas and others to small plots of land, and encouraged them to engage in Euro-American farming practices rather than hunting bison for subsistence. These tactics greatly limited the extent to which many communities could continue their previous food and therefore cultural practices. Out of these restrictions, however, new traditions (including the delicious tradition of making frybread) developed. Since the near-destruction of the bison population, public and private forces have helped to re-grow the population. Many Indigenous communities are today seeking to re-learn food traditions that were targeted during this era of Euro-American assimilation.

When we consider such ways that powerful governmental forces (themselves, of course, always made up of various and competing factions, like any group) have sought to shape and limit the ways of life of marginalized groups, we can better understand why some groups are fiercely concerned with self-determination, and fiercely argue for the right to control their own cultural practices and determine their own identities – sometimes by means of what they eat.

Sarah E. Dees completed her PhD at Indiana University in 2015. She is a scholar of American and Indigenous religions with a primary focus on representations, deployments, and theories of religion from the nineteenth century to the present day. Her research and teaching examine the relationship among religion, race, science, popular culture, and politics.

# 15. Who Are You? I'm an Alabamian

**Russell T. McCutcheon**

When, back in early 2001, I got the job as Chair of the Department of Religious Studies at the University of Alabama I was working at what was then called Southwest Missouri State University, in Springfield, MO (now Missouri State), and I recall sending out an email to my friends and colleagues in North America and Europe, to let them know that I'd soon be moving. Many wrote back their congratulations, of course, but I noticed a curious thing: unlike my Canadian and European friends, many of my US colleagues' congratulations came with what I read as subtle qualifications, equivocations, maybe even an unwritten sigh or two. For, sooner or later, they'd write something like, "Alabama? Really?" or "Wow. Well…, good luck."

It seemed that while others had read the part about becoming a department chair or moving to a major state university (from being an Assistant Professor at a regional state university), others couldn't get past the part about moving to Alabama.

Maybe it's just me, but I read those replies as laments – laments driven by a caricature of the state where I was moving to work. Now, fifteen years later, I guess I'm an Alabamian (to whatever degree those who have been here longer than me will allow me to claim that identity, that is – for there's an old joke in the South that the only thing worse than a northerner who moves south is one who stays), for, other than having lived in my childhood town until I was nineteen, I've lived here longer than anywhere else in my adult life. So I've got a few thoughts on how a certain idea of Alabama – one that is certainly not divorced from history but one which nonetheless is quite rhetorically useful today – helps others in the US to feel rather good about themselves (not unlike how some of us in "the South" use Mississippi's last-place finish on some national measures to soften the blow of our own poor showing on those very same reports).

For, from my point of view – as a Canadian who came to the US in 1993 for what was then only a nine-month teaching position, but which ended up turning into a whole career, at three different public universities (so far) – moving to Alabama wasn't all that significant. By then I'd almost lost count of how many different cities I'd lived in, whether in Canada or the US; and, besides, as a Canadian coming to the US back then at least, the main difference seemed to be defined by the US/Canada border at Fort Erie/Buffalo or at Windsor/Detroit (the two where we would cross), rather than any of the other differences defined by boundaries within the US itself. After all, despite an overwhelming number of pretty obvious similarities with Canada, once you crossed into the US the health care system was different (I'd never even heard of such a thing as "pre-existent conditions"), the gun laws were different ("Gun Control is a Steady Hand" said the bumper sticker on a truck in Knoxville), the banking and mortgage industries were regulated differently (did you notice that the 2008 real estate collapse didn't hit Canada anywhere near like it did the US...?), the tax system was different (I thought government's job was to redistribute wealth to the benefit of society...), the education system was different (property values linked to the quality of neighborhood schools? Seriously?!), and..., I could go on and on, of course. So although I'd seen *Smokey and the Bandit* (1977) and certainly knew that crossing state lines could be a big deal (if you had alcohol or minors in the car), once I'd crossed into the US then moving from Tennessee to Missouri and then on to Alabama didn't strike me as that much of a big deal.

Sure, I'd not lived in Manhattan or Seattle or San Francisco, to name but three other places, or any number of generally agreed upon cool or hip or whatever places in the US, but what counted as a difference to me, distinguishing my idea of home from this new place I'd moved to in order to pursue my career, was uniformly shared *by all places in the US*, suggesting that any local distinctions – no matter how significant they were to those who considered themselves connoisseurs of regional nuance – were of little consequence to me.

So you can imagine how I feel when someone (invariably an enlightened left-of-center type) asks me (as they actually have), "What are you *doing* at a place like that?" or when I hear their inevitable "What's it like teaching Religious Studies in the South" question – as if the issues that we confront, such as the insider/outsider problem, are not present in pretty much every classroom and as if we all don't have excellent students in our classes, regardless the region. You know, come to think of it, everywhere I've so far lived in the US has, at some point, been described to me as "the buckle of the bible belt," suggesting to me that there's no belt, just buckle wherever you go. So why would the issues in my classes be any different from anyone else's? I've been lucky enough to have lectured all over the US and it's not like my approach to the study of the category religion is somehow commonsense there but not here.

But I certainly "get" that there are things associated with some parts of the country that do stand out, even to the casual observer.

For example, I was born in 1961, so although I lived in Canada I was more than familiar with *Time* and *Life* magazine photospreads on what was going on in the US South during the 1960s, such as coverage of the harsh May 1963 response to civil rights protestors (that happened just prior to when I first began paging through those glossy American magazines, I realize) taking place in Birmingham, AL – now just an hour's drive away from where I live.

To this day I admit it's sobering to stop and think that I live right where much of this was all happening back then, those – I don't mind saying – deeply troubling images that, for me as a little boy, were nonetheless exotically alien, happenings in someone else's backyard, quite literally in a foreign land and thus a galaxy far, far away. So yes, of course, how can one live here without taking into account the deeply complex nature of what "Alabama" signifies for many people today – and for good reason.

And on my own campus we have the (in)famous doorway to Foster Auditorium in which our then Governor George Wallace (famously pictured with his arms behind his back, looking a tad defiant) stood, also in 1963, in order to try to prevent (and, because President Kennedy had federalized the Alabama National Guard, he failed) the first African-American students from registering at the University of Alabama – a door not so far from my office and one that I routinely take visitors to see, either letting their own memories inform their act of standing in that very same spot or, for younger guests, framing it with reference to a particular scene they may recall from *Forrest Gump* (1994).

So with regard to the history of its civil rights movement, the state of Alabama in general, and even the University of Alabama in particular, are undoubtedly (and rightly) on the tips of many people's tongues. But these issues go back further in time than the 1960s, of course; in fact, a couple of our faculty regularly do alternative campus tours with their students, in which they discuss the slave history of our own campus.

But all this being on the tips of people's tongues is a curious thing, for the pervasive beginnings and effects of slavery as an institution in the US, and the socio-political issues being addressed by the mid-twentieth-century civil rights movement, were hardly isolated to the state of Alabama or even to "the South." And here is where my analysis starts coming back around to the social effect of those laments that greeted the news of my impending move to Alabama: for although easily identified today as "a Southern problem," both were (and remain) national, even international, issues that impacted and implicated many more people than just the ancestors of those living where I happen to now.

Case in point, consider this new story on how Wisconsin – not Alabama but *Wisconsin* – is the worst state in the US for black children:

> Black families pondering a move to the Midwest might want to read this, especially if they have young children. According to a national report, Wisconsin has ranked the worst state in the country when it comes to racial disparities for children.

> The Annie E. Casey Foundation, a 66-year old charitable orga-
> nization concentrating on family issues and well-being, spear-
> headed the study. "Race for Results: Building to Opportunity
> for all Children" scored states according to 12 different fac-
> tors, from educational access to socioeconomic status and
> home life.

> Wisconsin scored a 238 on its ability to prepare black chil-
> dren for educational and financial success, the lowest of all
> states (the average score was 345). Interestingly, Wisconsin
> was ranked 10th overall in its preparation for white children.[1]

What's more, even the Canada I referenced above was hardly an
idyllic, tolerant, inclusive setting (as some might portray it); maybe
for a little boy looking at *Life* magazine it seemed to be, helping
me to feel safely set apart from (aka superior to) all those American
problems down south, but looking back we were surely as deeply
mired in much the same issues. While it wouldn't take much effort
to draw attention to longstanding (and still current) problems in
Canada over not recognizing native claims and rights, just the fact
that I can remember, also as a little boy, the first family moving
into my neighborhood who had obvious ancestry from Africa should
tell you all you need to know about the no less complex dynamics
of race, identity, and immigration taking place in "the Great White
North" (as we used to call it – never really catching the curiously
racial overtones to the apparent reference to snow).

So if we start to see these identity and power issues as hardly
local, then I'd hazard a guess that without decades of subsidy by
way of coerced labor (i.e., what we know as slavery), we would not
be wearing cotton much of the time today (i.e., what *was* slavery's
role in creating, by means of a massive subsidy of labor costs, what
is now a worldwide industry? What *does* one make of the flourishing northern textile industry then, and the so-called Industrial

1 See http://mic.com/articles/87933/this-is-the-worst-state-in-america-
for-black-children#.IUaQVjzNG, posted April 18, 2014 (accessed February
1, 2016).

Revolution that grew up around processing Southern-grown cotton? Not to mention the still flourishing tobacco industry, the sugar industry, the...). So, instead of documenting, for example, the evils of slavery here in the South, where it is relatively easily done (and needs to be done, of course), why not find its strategically unaddressed traces in those seemingly enlightened places where people – to my way of thinking, at least – all too easily judge what it means to live in Alabama?

For example, consider Julia Ott's post, entitled "Slaves: The Capital that Made Capitalism," which opens:

> Racial chattel slaves were *the* capital that made *capitalism*. While most theories of capitalism set slavery apart, as something utterly distinct, because under slavery, workers do not labor for a wage, new historical research reveals that for centuries, a single economic system encompassed both the plantation and the factory.[2]

But doing this, making that deeply self-implicating move, by seeing our entire, shared, taken-for-granted socio-economic system as deeply implicated, from top to bottom, would require us to realize that we're all in much the same soup, none of us all that removed from fiftieth place on any particular list – for issues and challenges of power, race, and place are found everywhere, making the luxury some have of thinking it's only a problem *here* and not *there* something that's bought at the price of seeing only others as the subjects of history. That is a luxury we do not have here – and I'm thankful for it. For it gives us little choice but to make sense today of the past that, like it or not, we've inherited.

So, while knowing that there's a number of things here that I would like to see change – as I would anywhere, believe me! – I also know that there's a number of people here doing what I consider to be admirable things, such as stepping up and naming that which

2 Posted at http://www.publicseminar.org/2014/04/slavery-the-capital-that-made-capitalism/#.WG6Fv33_SXk on April 9, 2014 (accessed February 1, 2016). Italics in the original.

often goes unaddressed. In fact, a student in our own department did that, in a prominent way, not that long ago, and was therefore among those who caught the attention of our University's administration, prompting it to begin moving more earnestly toward living up to our own statements on race and inclusion. So more changes are now happening. Yes, it's slow, frustratingly slow at times, sure, but Rome wasn't built in a day either.

So while I certainly wish some things were otherwise – yes, I admit that I side with Neil Young over Lynyrd Skynyrd (listen to the back and forth in their songs to figure out that reference) – there's plenty of people here who make me proud to live in Alabama and to teach at the University of Alabama – sentiments that are especially apparent to me whenever I bump into those who live in no less complex places but who nonetheless feel competent to judge us, based on a convenient caricature that they think inoculates them from the effects of our shared history.

So there ya go: that's what I'm doing in a place like this. And that's who I am.

Russell T. McCutcheon is Professor and Chair of the Department of Religious Studies at the University of Alabama. He has published widely on the study of religion's history and the politics of classification – specifically the socio-political uses of the taxon "religion" (whether employed as a folk or technical term).

# 16. Secrecy, Stories, and Boundaries

## Emily A. Schmidt

Russell McCutcheon's reflection on being an Alabamian centers on the way non-Alabamians understand, depict, and caricature the people and political climate of the state. The bulk of his piece addresses his childhood perceptions of the US, perceptions of Alabama by outsiders, and the reality those perceptions are based on. In other words, much of his reflection on identity is centered on what Alabama's *not*. The identity work in his piece is not accomplished by explaining what makes him feel connected to the place "Alabama" or by describing the cultural elements (like values, music, or food) he shares with other "Alabamians."

Identity is constructed, at least in part, by creating boundaries around ourselves, as individuals or as groups, that make *us* insiders and *them* outsiders. The creation of categories helps us to organize our images, understandings, or perceptions of the world and our role/s within that world. In describing the way others reacted to the news of his accepting a job and moving to Alabama, McCutcheon reports receiving qualified or equivocating congratulations from his US colleagues. They'd congratulate him on the job, but express a certain amount of horror at the idea of someone *actually moving to Alabama.* Many people who live in the US have an image of Alabama – whether they've been there or not – that is, as he writes, a caricature. A caricature of an individual works by emphasizing some obvious and distinguishing physical characteristic, like Jay Leno's big chin or Barack Obama's big ears, to stand as uniquely identifying of that person. Likewise, common caricatures of Alabama pick out identifiable aspects of the state's socio-political and cultural history (for example, racism and related issues) and emphasize them *as if they are* uniquely identifying characteristics of Alabama, or even of "the South."

By treating racism as a "Southern thing," or more specifically, as an "Alabama thing," this caricature McCutcheon describes allows people who use this image to mark racism as unique to those states in "the South." McCutcheon points this out in his piece, noting that the racism and related socio-political issues that typically shape the caricature of Alabama or "the South" are not isolated to that state or even to the region. Rather, they are issues that permeate US culture and institutions. Yet when outsiders deploy this caricature, they establish racism as the identifiable characteristic of *someplace else* and *someone else*. Racism becomes beliefs, actions, and social structures *that happen in other places*, and that *other people* believe, do, and establish or participate in. Use of this caricature therefore defines both geographical and cultural boundaries: *They* do that *over there* but *we* don't do it *here*. This construction of otherness makes it easy to criticize the perceived problems of other groups while feeling better about one's own social group.

In order for this technique to successfully distinguish "them" from "us" in this case (and probably in many other cases) insiders must believe that the distinction they're making does, in fact, exist. What if, as in the case of the caricature of Alabama, the distinction is not so clear? What if "we" do, in fact, do what "they" do? The caricature of Alabama only does the identity work its users want it to do if they consciously ignore, or are otherwise unaware, of the problem at a national level or in their own state. What if we instead start from a position that maintains that the US has a longstanding, national problem with racism? If every state has it then it's structural and systemic. A few examples should suffice: displacement of and violence towards Native Americans, the enslavement of Africans and segregation of their descendants, the internment of Japanese and Japanese Americans, and recent calls to deny Muslims entrance into the US. These few examples have lasting effects on the social and economic locations of these peoples – suggesting that seeing racism as only *their* problem may not be as accurate as we sometimes think, for it requires us to overlook how it may also shape our own world.

Michael Taussig calls this type of conscious ignoring "knowing what not to know" and the thing being ignored a "public secret" (Taussig 1999: 1–8). The public secret "can be defined as *that which is generally known but cannot be articulated*" (ibid.: 5; italics in the original). Santa Claus is one of his examples: although it's generally known that Santa Claus is not real, it's considered rude or mean-spirited to say so openly – especially around children. There's a sense that part of the transition from childhood to adulthood, and thus to full membership within the community, consists of learning the secret, and learning that "we" don't talk about it (ibid.: 267–71).[1] When the public secret is something even more culturally significant than Santa Claus, articulating the secret may have greater social consequences. By keeping the illusion that we do not know the public secret, societal norms and ideals are reinforced inasmuch as they remain unchallenged. For once the secret is publicly revealed, societal norms and ideals are scrutinized, leading to social change or to the reification and re-secreting of the secret, or both.

When he articulates the history of slavery in the US and connects it to contemporary Wisconsin, McCutcheon draws attention to the public secret that racism and related socio-economic problems are national rather than regional. Once the secret has been revealed, the caricature of Alabama and Alabamians no longer functions effectively because it has been revealed that these problems are not unique to Alabama. In my reading, McCutcheon's articulation of this public secret is also a call to action for social change, through the development of "alternative histories" that name this secret and that identify steps to eliminate racism. McCutcheon's self-identification as an Alabamian does not deny that racism is a problem in Alabama, but places it in the larger context of US history.

---

1 The example of Santa Claus, in the context of the US, points to the predominance of Christian cultural practices here. Even practitioners of other religious traditions, or of no religious tradition, are subject to the social rules of this public secret.

The public secret of slavery and racism in the US can now be understood as a critical element of the collective identity of the nation. Americans have idealized the US to represent freedom and equality in founding documents like the Constitution, in holidays like Independence Day, in legendary stories about the nation's founders, and in propagandistic songs like the national anthem. In recent response to the deaths of black people and failures to indict or convict the killers, Alicia Garza (@aliciagarza), Patrisse Cullors (@osope), and Opal Tometi (@opalayo) began the Twitter hashtag #blacklivesmatter, registered the Twitter handle @Blklivesmatter, and are among the founders of the associated movement.[2] People involved with the movement have used cell phone videos to document the behavior of the officers involved and have called for institutional reforms to address the inequalities that grew out of the national history of slavery and racism.[3] Thus, the articulation of the public secret has resulted in critique of social norms.

Calling attention to the ways the nation has failed to produce equality often results in denial: re-hiding the secret behind claims of the greatness of America and rejecting the person (or people) reminding society of the secret it would rather ignore. Critics of the Black Lives Matter movement deny the revelation of the public secret and re-secret current events and history. They emphasize the role of the police in public safety to deflect improper action away from the shooters and onto the people who were killed, suggesting that if only the dead had behaved appropriately the police wouldn't have had to kill them. They emphasize the rights of all people to freedom of speech, the end of legally enforced segregation, and the end of anti-miscegenation laws as counter-proof to the evidence for the long-term, continued ramifications of slavery and racism on African-Americans. As a result, the public secret, somewhat ironically perhaps, is re-secreted and reified by a renewed emphasis on

2 See https://twitter.com/hashtag/BlackLivesMatter, and http://blacklivesmatter.com/ (accessed September 21, 2016),

3 See https://policy.m4bl.org/platform/ for one statement of the movement's platform (accessed September 21, 2016).

the often-cited ideals of freedom and equality in America – which are re-presented as if they are inherent to the nation.

Moreover, public secrets are often related to, or hidden by stories (or histories) told in ways that omit or conceal the information that would reveal them. Margaret Somers (1994) argues that people understand themselves and interpret their experiences within the context of a story or stories. Identity is constructed as individuals or communities place themselves within and interpret their experiences through stories. In fact, McCutcheon alludes to this in his piece when he not only tells us a story himself, of moving to Alabama, but also when he mentions that some University of Alabama faculty lead "alternative campus tours…in which they discuss the slave history of [the] campus." Alternative histories respond to and establish changes in identity, in part by articulating the public secret. Rather than concealing the slave-holding history of the campus or the nation, alternative narratives of history shift the boundaries of collective identity by including people and experiences that were concealed or omitted in previous narratives. The acts of concealing or revealing public secrets and telling or changing stories are among a number of techniques for building boundaries and creating identity.

McCutcheon's claim to be Alabamian is therefore a claim that connects him as an individual to a larger group of people, implying that he shares something in common with other Alabamians – something that, it turns out, people in the state may share with people far beyond the state's borders. This identity claim centers on the relationships between an individual and a group, as well as a connection between a group and a place. These three aspects of identity construction are interdependent and mutually reinforcing, since humans exist as individuals, within groups, and within a place. McCutcheon's self-identification as an Alabamian therefore connects him to the people (Alabamians) who live in the same place he lives (Alabama). Ultimately, this self-identification is about connecting to other people and establishing his place (geographically and socially) as an Alabamian, in spite of the possibility that native Alabamians might always identify him as a Canadian. Yet in all of these identifications, the boundaries between *me* and *you*, *us* and *them*, are constructed, maintained, and sometimes challenged, at least in part, by the secrets that we keep or reveal in the stories that we tell.

# References

Somers, Margaret R. (1994). "The Narrative Constitution of Identity: A Relational and Network Approach." *Theory and Society* 25(3): 605–49. https://doi.org/10.1007/BF00992905

Taussig, Michael (1999). *Defacement: Public Secrecy and the Labor of the Negative*. Stanford: Stanford University Press.

Emily A. Schmidt is a doctoral candidate in Religious Studies, with an emphasis on the Ancient Mediterranean, at the University of California, Santa Barbara. Her research interests include religions in the Roman Empire, archaeology of religion, and construction of religious identities.

# 17. Who Are You? I'm Vaia and I'm Touna

## Vaia Touna

Who we are comes with a name and mine is Vaia, or better said, Vaia Touna. I was baptized Vaia (Βαΐα in Greek, pronounced Va-ee-a) but family and friends would call me Vaya (as in *Vaya con dios*), that is, until I got into university when I decided that Vaia sounded more professional; besides, that was the name written on my Identification Card, so friends from the university years and on know me as Vaia.

It's interesting that the name that we come to think is so much part of who we are was chosen and given to us by others, most likely by our parents. Who we are and how we perceive ourselves is certainly socially constructed, for there is nothing in the name that I was given that corresponds to some essential core of "me"; think about how much teaching and training was involved until I learned to respond to this specific name, Vaya, and how much I had to train others (myself included) to call me Vaia when I made the switch, yet it is impossible now to think of myself as anything but Vaia.

I also realize that when I introduce myself I stress my first name rather than my last; somehow that is how I recognize myself, I am Vaia more than I am Touna. I remember years ago I was at a lecture in Aristotle University, in Thessaloniki, Greece, organized by one of my Professors (Ioannis Petrou) and after the lecture I was introduced to the speaker (given that I was on the planning committee for that lecture), Christos Yannaras, a very well-known theologian and Greek Orthodox philosopher in Greece. Yannaras, upon hearing my first name, gave me a lecture on how it was "grammatically incorrect." My name Vaia means "Palm Sunday's leaves" which is always plural and therefore the correct name would be its plural form, that is, Vaya and not the singular form, Vaia. Despite the fact that his argument made sense (though I thought it was a bit weird), for some reason the fact that my name "Vaia" was a "grammatical error" made it even more appealing for me to use. My own rebellion? "Whatever…"

Years later I came to Edmonton, Canada, to pursue a PhD in Religious Studies. One summer I visited a very famous heritage festival, held in one of Edmonton's parks. The festival hosts countries from almost all over the world and they each have a stand where you can be acquainted with the culture of the country. Of course, I visited the Greek booth and before I knew it I was being introduced to the people of Edmonton's local Greek community. Curiously enough, as they met me and learned my name, they too were each correcting it from Vaia to Vaya. Why would it matter to them how I say my name? What was at stake there? By then, of course, I was able to defend my choice, taking recourse to a variety of strategic moves, ultimately saying that I had been baptized Vaia, which seemed to be the final convincing argument from my end, "'cause who can defy the Church?" In light of that incident, though, my previous encounter with the professor in Thessaloniki made a bit more sense, illustrating the sort of policing that happens and the kind of strategies we use for certain interests and identification processes; Yannaras invoked "proper Greek grammar" in order to convince me, while I invoked "the Greek Orthodox church" in order to convince the members of the Greek community – which may tell you a lot about the two main policing authorities of Greek identity, the language (and whoever masters that) and the orthodox church.

But here is another interesting moment in name politics that I should recount. During that festival I was asked by the people of the Greek community to teach Greek to a class of seven- to eight-year-olds, which of course I was happy to do. One student's name was Athena; immediately for me that was the name of the goddess of wisdom. Now, I have to explain for my non-Greek readers that, in Greek, Athena (Αθηνα), with a slight difference in intonation, can be both the name of the city Αθήνα (pronounced Atheena with the stress on "ee") and also the name of the goddess Αθηνά (pronounced Athenaa with the stress being on the last "aa"); so although they are written the same a small change in the intonation and they are not only pronounced differently but they mean two different things.

Now, when my student introduced herself to me she said Αθήνα (the name of the city), which I perceived as a mistake, given that her knowledge of Greek was very limited; but it also spoke of my own assumptions about the Greek diaspora. So for a couple of weeks I kept correcting her and explaining the proper pronunciation, that is, Αθηνά (the name of the goddess). Then one time after the class was over, I met with her mother and we had a friendly talk about Athena's progress in class, in the course of which her mother referred to Athena as Αθήνα (that is, the name of the city). Of course I didn't miss the opportunity to correct the mother as well, only to hear, to my surprise, that their daughter was actually named after the city and not the goddess. I felt really embarrassed, because I had failed to realize that although in Greece it would indeed be unlikely for parents to name their child after a Greek city, being in Canada it made perfect sense for second- or third-generation Greeks to name their child after a city with such an ancient and renowned history and civilization that they would consider part of their heritage. Besides, Athena (Αθήνα) was born around the time of the 2004 Olympic Games in Athens and, as the mother told me, that was what inspired her and her husband to give the name of the city to their daughter.

This is pretty much the sort of problem that arises when we take our local categories, classifications, and understandings to be universal. But also, it speaks of the circle of policing around the proper way to use, in this case, Greek names, and I guess the way we also police being Greek, something that we all do and, in so doing, authenticate ourselves as the proper representatives of "Greek naming." Yannaras and other members of the Greek community did it to me, and I did it to my student and her parents – all interesting name arm-wrestling matches.

But how about my last name? You hardly ever hear your last name growing up – that is, people hardly ever will address you with it, until of course high school – and then you see it printed in official documents and you use it to sign various papers so it feels too "official" perhaps. It certainly does not feel as much "you" as your first name, I suppose, because family and friends would hardly ever address you with it, so you are not familiarized with it (or at least I am not). For example, in April of 2014 I found myself at a conference at Lehigh University, being one among six presenters on the topic of "Code Switching," and during a break I was standing with Monica Miller – who was the host of the conference and also a presenter herself. We were approached by a student who introduced herself to me, and instantly both Monica and I introduced myself. Now, given that at the time I was still a grad student (you are not yet a scholar but you are not a student either in the strict sense of the word; it's a liminal phase), I felt a certain kind of familiarity with the student and said "Vaia," while Monica said "Touna." Somehow at this moment, in that context, "Touna" seemed more appropriate given that I was a presenter and soon to hold a PhD. So I thought to myself, "Right, I am Touna," and at that moment I think I was one step further along the way becoming a scholar. And now that I have finished my PhD I see the training and time it takes to get used to being "Dr Touna" or "Professor Touna."

It was interesting that the conference I was attending was on code switching. It should be evident in all of the above examples how we are constantly changing between codes we use (Vaia/Vaya, Vaia/Touna, Atheena/Athenaa), even if it is just the names that identify ourselves, and there are many things at stake in how we do this (or elect not to). In other words, our names are not neutral descriptions and representations of who we are; for, depending on how we introduce ourselves or how we are referred to by others, they may be indicative of interests, agendas and implications, whether we think about it or not, that have social consequences.

Vaia Touna is Assistant Professor at the Department of Religious Studies at the University of Alabama. Her interests range widely, from looking at specific concepts of religion in the Greco-Roman world and methodological issues concerning the study of religion in general, to focusing on processes of identification with examples drawn from Ancient and Modern Greece. She is now working on a book tentatively titled *Fabrication of the Greek Past: Religion, Tradition, and Modern Identities*.

# 18. "Naaaaaw, You Show Me YOUR ID"

## Richard Newton

Something as liberating as using one's own name is bound by a great number of institutional obligations. In the previous chapter, Vaia Touna has shown how names come with "interests, agendas, and implications…that have social consequences." She describes learning to navigate "the circle of policing" that protects and serves those who claim to know who she really is.

Through various encounters, Vaia Touna came to understand her own name as an index of "the two main policing authorities of Greek identity, the language…and the orthodox church." "Vaia" was grammatically incorrect until she baptized it in the Greek Orthodox Church. "Touna" was standoffish until she professed her academic pedigree. Once she identified the terms on which her name said what she needed it to say, she could move freely in those spaces…just as long as her name met the conditions of those on guard.

The social theorist Louis Althusser (2014: 191) expressed this conundrum as *interpellation*. He maintained that who we are is not as simple as naming ourselves but the product of competing social entities invested in naming who we are. Althusser similarly invoked the example of a police action, one as innocuous as an officer yelling, "Hey, you there!" As Russell McCutcheon notes in the introduction to this volume, interpellation registers the social psychological pull that compels us to guiltily turn, just in case we are unknowingly suspicious.

Vaia Touna felt this pull when seeing the futility of her Identification Card. If possessing an ID card could really settle the matter of who she is, then Vaia could have taken comfort in her first name without concern for her professional academic rank: "besides, that was the name written on my Identification Card." Likewise there was something all too "official" about Touna owning the last name "printed in official documents" and used "to sign various papers." It was as if she didn't want to overstate or press her case too far. So what good then is an Identification Card if it doesn't work in the owner's favor?

While Touna was surfacing these power dynamics around the site of Greek ethnicity, I could not help but think about an ID card being like an Ouija board where an invisible hand spells out a revealing message. When we shift our understanding of identity to a series of "operational acts of identification" (Bayart 2005: 92), we can appreciate the conspicuous production of the credentialing talisman. Interpellation names the rough edges of our smoothest fabrications – the cultural formations to which we never give a second thought. It reveals even our most effortless gestures to be forced.

An ID card documents the current state of negotiations between the holder and the issuing authority. It warrants possessors' to reconsider their accountability to the issuing authority in a given moment. To ask for another's identification is to claim the power to verify not only *who* belongs but also *to whom* they belong. Here I can't help but see resonances with African-Americans' indenture to the so-called "race card," a pejorative description for pointing out racialized seams in the United States' integrated banner.

A story from a black, Houston rapper by the name of Nosaprise immediately comes to mind. Also known as Nosa Edebor, his Facebook page records a friend's entanglement with the police at a bus stop. The cop believed himself to have probable cause to investigate whether Edebor's *urban* friend had failed in some unnamed compliance. When the suspect was asked to produce identification, he replied, "Naaaaaw, you show me your ID." Edebor withholds the aftermath for comedic effect, but the excerpt gives us pause to interrogate how identity is policed.

If the cop really wanted demographic information about Edebor's friend, then a much different conversation would have ensued. The incident was about something more. The officer was reminding the suspect of the order of things – namely, who was in charge of the streets. Does the police action befit the authority of a bona fide state officer, or does it undermine a sworn duty to the state's citizens? The intent becomes clearer when the accused mimics the tactic to reciprocate the claim of authority. Black history is a dramatization – if not a cautionary tale – about questioning how identification works.

In the 1977 American mini-series *Roots*, a recently captured African refuses to stay put on his master's quarters (Kunta Kinte 2011). After a failed attempt to gain freedom, the runaway is captured and whipped by a slave-breaker, tasked with teaching blacks to obey their masters. All the quartered slaves stand by, watching the beating and and hearing the screaming. The downbeats alternate with an accented verse, "What's your name?" with the slave replying, "Kunta Kinte." Everyone in the scene knows how to end the torture. Kunta Kinte simply has to answer with the right name…, his slave name…, his Christian name, "Toby." The exchange goes on long enough for audiences on both sides of the screen to locate their own empathy. Were Kunta to identify as Toby, the present physical torture would end. But as long as he identifies himself as Kunta, a part of him remains out of the slave institution's hands. Ultimately Kunta succumbs to the slave-breaker and says, "Toby," just before falling out of consciousness.

To what extent might identity be described as a cessation of consciousness at the hands of an authority? The question does not nullify the notion of agency, but observes that ID cards mark the limits at which declarations of independence become anything but self-evident. Anthropologist Ronald L. Grimes (2000: 94) is hard-pressed to identify a modern Western rite of passage, but he names adolescent receipt of the driver's license as the best example. I think this is an appropriate analogy given its underlying conceit. The laminated paper does not make one more capable of turning a key. It does, however, codify an agreement to move according to a set of prescribed motoring laws under legal penalty. Furthermore, it signifies that the reader's interpretation of those laws will henceforth be adjudicated by the state. Freedom is the ironic reward of rule-followers.

The example of the drivers' license seems harmless enough – a tool to keep children and the otherwise-incapable from something so dangerous as auto-mobility. After all, who doesn't want safe roadways? Yet a similar paternalistic ableism accompanied the issuance of American marriage licenses. In the nineteenth century, the United States (especially – but not solely – in the South) used these documents to identify who was unfit for the privilege of matrimony – a category that barred slave betrothal, incest, polygamy, miscegenation, and same-sex marriage. Without regulation unions could lead to abominable procreation – among other activities – that would throw the social order in disarray. Over time, the United States has amended some of its restrictions. For instance, the 2015 *Obergefell v. Hodges* US Supreme Court ruling compels states to license and recognize same-sex marriages under the due process and equal protection clauses of the Constitution. As precedent, this decision cited the 1967 case *Loving v. Virginia*, which legalized interracial marriage. But let us not forget that these progressive decisions also increase the purview of those seeking government oversight of actions they might otherwise have done themselves. One is "made an honest (wo)man" by seeking the court's blessing and adding to its authority. Interpellation preempts the pull of police action by inviting authorities to sanction the marriage from the start.

Many African-American parents home-school their children on best practices in self-identifying as an upstanding, law-abiding citizen. The curriculum includes cautionary tales about police officers requesting suspects to show identification and then mistaking the requisite gesture for drawing a weapon. Case in point, in 2014, white, South Carolina State Trooper Sean Groubert pled guilty for shooting thirty-five-year-old Levar Jones in a representative incident (Crimesider Staff 2016). The pull of interpellation informs strategies like the one described by actor LeVar Burton in a cable news discussion on the criminalization of blackness. To comprehend the sting of his critique, it is worth noting that Burton portrayed the young Kunta Kinte in *Roots*.

> Listen, I'm gonna be honest with you, and this is a practice I engage in every time I'm stopped by law enforcement. And I taught this to my son who is now 33 as part of my duty as a father to ensure that he knows the kind of world in which he is growing up. So when I get stopped by the police, I take my hat off and my sunglasses off, I put them on the passenger's side, I roll down my window, I take my hands, I stick them outside the window and on the door of the driver's side because I want that officer to be relaxed as possible when he approaches my vehicle. And I do that because I live in America. (CNN 2013)

Self-policing is not unique to African-Americans or to anyone feeling the pull of identification. ID cards ticket entry into a panoptical world, a prison where the inmates are under constant surveillance (UCL Bentham Project n.d.). Burton gives voice to what so many forget. Jones reminds us how some cannot afford to do so.

In an era when the nation struggles to determine whether and how much black lives matter, I think it fair to say that the instances above are not extraordinary. And yet the legitimating politics of this racialized conflict are most scrupulous in the empty ID cards wherein we write ourselves. I've observed this in myself and other African-Americans when traveling abroad. We come to the border agent who provides the form, dictating everything but the terms of our surrender – first name, last name, and so on. One of the boxes asks for ethnicity, and for so many of us there's a pause. There simply are not enough spaces to address "the Negro question." And no matter what one does to force that racial history into the box, the writing will say something like "American." Customs sees to it that your handiwork effaces the evidence of the invisible pull behind your pen strokes. And all appears well until someone stops you and says, "American?! Naaaaaw, you show me YOUR ID."

# References

Althusser, Louis (2014 [1971]). *On the Reproduction of Capitalism: Ideology and Ideological State Apparatuses*. Trans. G.M. Goshgarian. New York: Verso.

Bayart, Jean-François (2005 [1996]). *The Illusion of Cultural Identity*. Trans. Stenven Rendall, Janet Roitman, Cynthia Schoch, and Jonathan Derrick. Chicago: University of Chicago Press.

CNN (2013). Burton: "I put hands outside car when pulled over." https://www.youtube.com/watch?v=M-ckDJ3xTaE. (accessed May 15, 2016).

Crimesider Staff (2016). White S.C. Trooper Pleads Guilty in Shooting of Unarmed Black Man. http://www.cbsnews.com/news/white-south-carolina-trooper-pleads-guilty-in-shooting-of-unarmed-black-man-levar-jones/ (accessed May 15, 2016).

Grimes, Ronald L. (2000). *Deeply into the Bone: Re-inventing Rites of Passage*. Berkeley: University of California Press.

Kunta Kinte (2011). "Your name is TOBY! What's your name?" https://www.youtube.com/watch?v=1CpJpGF8lS8 (accessed May 15, 2016).

UCL Bentham Project (n.d). The Panopticon. https://www.ucl.ac.uk/Bentham-Project/who/panopticon (accessed May 15, 2016).

Richard Newton is Assistant Professor of Religious Studies at Elizabethtown College. His research focuses on the anthropology of scriptures. He also curates *Sowing the Seed*, an online student-scholar magazine on religion, culture, and teaching. See his work at sowingtheseed.org.

# 19. Who Are You? I'm a New Mom

## K. Merinda Simmons

Being a mother was never part of my general life plan. In fact, where babies are concerned, I'm the unsophisticated rube who tends to think all infants look, sound, and smell the same. So, when my partner and I learned we were going to be parents in just forty short weeks (that's another thing – even now, the week count might as well be military time, as far as I'm concerned), we traded blank stares regarding what that means or how to go about thinking toward how our lives would change once the squirmy, cartilage-laden fellow joined us.

We did what any startled academics might do when confronting something unexpected: we gathered information, and fast. Pregnancy became a project through which I could exorcise some data-driven control issues. If I *knew* enough, I'd *do* enough.

A funny thing happened as I pored over the must-read books from all sorts of different schools of thought promoting a particular method as *the way* to be pregnant, to deliver a baby, and to subsequently rear said baby…. While there were and remain vast disagreements over how one might go about being a mother, one claim seemed paramount pretty much across the board: motherhood is, so many authors suggested, a mantle one adopts by tapping into an intrinsic Ur-mom identity held deep within oneself. One book I found useful while thinking toward my own labor and delivery, for example, is *Birthing from Within* (Partera Press, 1998). It's got a lot of cool information in it, such as a discussion of informed consent for pregnant women, pain-coping mechanisms, and strategies for transitioning into caring for a newborn. It's also a text whose author describes the end of her labor process as follows: "for an unforgettable moment…I felt a oneness with all mothers who had ever given birth, and to mothers all over the world who were laboring and giving birth with me that night…I had become a link in the eternal chain of Mothers."

Maybe this supposed universality is why so many women suddenly began tilting their heads and smirking at me, asking how I was "hanging in" – as if I was a neophyte in the midst of a kindly hazing en route to my status as insider. This seeming clear and present identity space, however, is something that requires a very specific set of performances. That is, the series of acts I performed from the time a bump began to emerge seemed to suggest the degree of my success (or lack thereof) in gaining access to the transcendent realm of Motherhood.

I'll offer the punch line first. I never ended up owning a crib. My kid – now two years old – never "cried out" anything. The delicate balance of keeping him happy and getting work done often resulted during his infancy (and still does, occasionally) in his being carried around in a sling or wrap that leaves my hands free to load the dishwasher or work on essays. Feeding him has always worked according to supply and demand, which leaves us largely without any real schedule to speak of. We used cloth diapers, which seemed to save money and create less mess. There has never been a specific nursery space in the house. These matter-of-fact realities about how the domestic dance happened to emerge were and are not the result of intense deliberation on my part. Often, I'm not really thinking much about them at all. They are largely to do with my own very local interests where time, money, and energy are concerned.

But it's been amazing to learn how quickly these little actions classify me for many as an "Attachment Parent." And this, apparently, is to be immediately and strongly distinguished in diametric opposition to Authoritative Parenting or approaches that would promote a clear structure, like the Parent-Directed Feeding advocated in the wildly popular (or infamous, depending) *On Becoming Babywise* (Parent-wise Solutions, 2012).

Not too far into my pregnancy, I realized that the discourse on motherhood among insiders, while complicated and multifaceted, often plays out in my own communities through battles like: strollers v. slings, formula v. breastmilk, and cribs v. co-sleeping. And the accompanying judgments can be intense. I often felt like *30 Rock's* Liz Lemon, who, in a episode that particularly resonated with me, made the mistake of asking an online group of moms for suggestions about where to get "a girl's bike." The two initial responses she got go like this:

> "I'm sorry, what's a 'girl's bike? Is that like a 'girl' doctor? Go back to Saudi Arabia, Hitler!"

> "UR buying a bike but not a helmet? The head is where the child's brain is! Why don't you get educated, Double Hitler!"

Of course, these disagreements and delineations say as much about the commonalities among the various schools of thought as they do about their differences. For example, I have received advice from advocates of baby-wearing who offered slings and wraps as a way to avoid the strollers, which they believe to be less beneficial (some would say clearly terrible) for both children and mothers. The exact same conversations happen with moms who swear by their strollers – the tool of liberation for moms everywhere, they say – and who think slings are tantamount to foot-binding.

What these chats have in common is not only their ideological certainty but also their conservative assumption that mothers are the ones who will be doing the real child-rearing. It was a bitter pill to swallow for my interests in keeping up an active work life and maintaining a domestic division of labor. What's more, these conversations typically happened outside of work settings in the middle of a weekday. Why does that matter? Well, for many, being able to hang out with friends on a sunny Wednesday afternoon suggests a certain level of privilege that allows for a flexible work schedule or the ability to stay home altogether. So, depending on what kinds of qualities we're using to compare and contrast, my slinging and strolling friends might have way more in common with one another than, say, with women who make the same choice regarding baby-related mobility but whose professional or economic circumstances keep them at work during the day. These brief anecdotal moments are chock-full of particularities related to gender, class, and region, just to name a few.

Interestingly, though, these midday conversations are indicative of a discourse that *does* want to invoke the practices of women with very different contexts – often in different countries – in order to validate parenting styles of choice. In so doing, the very moms with whom I find myself agreeing on many issues – homebirth advocacy, baby-wearing, breastfeeding (if able) upon demand, etc. – often make use of a romanticized, exotic otherness to identify and defend specific interests within their performative spaces. All the while, my cohort is able to applaud itself for our progressive stance on matters being debated among parents in our specific communities, even as a logic structure remains up and running that suggests certain groups or practices are somehow closer to nature or more authentic than others. Thus, the promotion of certain ideas and issues thought not mainstream – perhaps even taboo – here in North America easily relies on cultural essentialism if one is not careful, deploying the notion of a shared, sacred and ancestral mothering impulse to do so. For example, I've come across several texts talking about African women who wrap their babies onto their own chests or backs so as to more easily continue working, performing chores, etc. One that especially struck me was a lengthy blog post entitled "Breastfeeding in Mongolia" on a site I typically quite like. The author's critique of North American norms that ostracize women breastfeeding in public or for longer than a year is well-taken. To make this critique, however, the author embarks upon a discussion of what Mongolians (presented as a unified mass group) do. The romanticized notion of a stable cultural identity is offered without question; the fact that it is cast in a complimentary light, however, makes it no less reductive.

In such examples (these are just a couple of many), the performance (wrapping or breastfeeding) is conveniently removed from the context in which women enact it. While my own new-mom identification carries with it a distaste for the stigma that often comes with public breastfeeding, my guess is that – rather than some monolith called "Mongolian women" having accessed that sacred ancestral mothering impulse that transcends time and space – there are probably practical and local reasons for longer-term breastfeeding in parts of Mongolia. Those pragmatics may or may not be part of the daily grind for attachment parents like "us." But that is not really the concern of resources aimed at helping women connect with that authentic Mother thought to be in us all.

The same brand of universalism then gets applied to infants as well. For instance, there's the undeniably adorable film *Babies* (Thomas Balmès, 2010), which follows the first year of four children (one each in Namibia, Mongolia, Japan, and the US). The script-free film was billed as a "universal celebration of the magic and innocence of babies." No dialogue needed. It is, instead, a photojournalistic feast on the order of the best in *National Geographic*-esque visual stimulation. Babies are babies everywhere! They navigate matters of food, shelter, and power/competition all over the world! Sure... but how those navigations play out and what meanings they're given vary widely. In fact, the very claim that infants play out a universal script is itself reflective of a quite particular context. So, while I (an introvert's introvert) suddenly feel okay about flashing a knowing look at a pregnant woman in a grocery check-out line or unabashedly asking other women about how they keep up their bodies' milk supplies, I process these phenomena of new motherhood through my own filter. Does my status as a mother connect me with all mothers everywhere? Well, that depends entirely on one's criteria used for comparison.

Speaking only for myself (isn't that all one can ever do?), when I see "Mother" with a capital "M", the first thing that comes to mind is Dan Aykroyd's affable conspiracy-theorist character with the groovy dance moves in the 1992 film *Sneakers*.

K. Merinda Simmons is Associate Professor of Religious Studies at the University of Alabama. She is editor of the Equinox series *Concepts in the Study of Religion: Critical Primers* and is currently working on a monograph tentatively entitled *Sourcing Slave Religion: Theorizing Experience in the American South* as well as two co-authored books: *Gender: A Critical Primer* (with Craig Martin) and *Race and New Modernisms* (with James A. Crank).

# 20. I'm a Soon-to-be Dad

## Jason W.M. Ellsworth

When I first received the offer to be part of the *Fabricating Identities* volume I was quite taken aback for three reasons. First, to be included in a project from the Culture on the Edge blog (which I follow regularly and recommend to many people) is something that I consider to be an honor. Second, I was asked to respond to K. Merinda Simmons' excellent blog post, "Who Are You? I'm a New Mom," and yet I am neither a mom nor a parent. There are two dogs that live in our house that we jokingly call our dauggers – though I would hardly say this is comparable to being a parent to a small human being. Finally, unbeknownst to the editor and most people at the time, my spouse was now pregnant, making this quite a coincidence.

How would I respond to this piece when I was not yet privy to the parent's "insider" view, making this a topic I was just beginning to explore (as a soon-to-be dad)? Perhaps this was a feeling that many of my fellow respondents in this volume asked themselves when first receiving the piece to which they would be responding. As someone who has a background in the study of religion, anthropology, and marketing what could I say about motherhood? And yet this is exactly what the tools of my trade, in the study of religion, have prepared me to do and what Simmons' article helps to display. For as Russell T. McCutcheon states:

> Making the discourse on religion one's data…entails questioning and examining apparent self-evidences and seeing methodological and theoretical consensus not simply as natural but as something that develops over time, is continually

encouraged and contested, and may at times even be manu-
factured, all in the context of historical, social, and political
factors. (1997: 7)

Making the discourse on religion the focus rather than a self-evident
religious ideal turns the gaze onto the present and who is trying
to direct the debate. It is what separates scholarship on the study
of religion from theology. This is what I find so illuminating about
Simmons' piece – that we (or, in this case, our discourse on motherhood) can become the data, and the task of the critical scholar is to
examine the construction of identity (i.e., motherhood) rather than
take it as self-evident. To do this, Simmons intertwines the biographical and theoretical analysis of what it means to be a "mother,"
constructing a short auto-ethnography of sorts to explore her own
constructed identity and place in a social spectrum. Simmons' examples of the "in" and "out" groups (parents versus non-parents; mothers versus non-mothers; stroller versus non-stroller moms), gives a
glimpse of the illusion of identity that Jean-François Bayart refers to
when stating "we identify ourselves less with respect to membership
in a community or a culture than with respect to the communities
and cultures with which we have relations" (2005: 95). It is not the
internal us that gives one an identity but our relations to others that
construct the category.

   Similar to Simmons' training to become a parent, as someone
who does not see babies on a regular basis I too have had to look
elsewhere for guidance. While there is the often-cited notion that it
takes a village to raise a child, there is no direct training with babies
in my "village." All of the children in our surrounding "village" go
to childcare, are at home with their parents, or exist outside the areas
I visit. While we may have socialist tendencies in Canada, where I
live, the individualistic, capitalist ideals permeate around us, keeping us separated and focused on keeping our bootstraps pulled up
so that we can get ahead in society. Or in other words, parents are
expected to be able to take care of their own children, work full-time
jobs, and live a fulfilling life without the help of the rest of society;
if one cannot, then one is a failed parent it seems.

As a PhD student in Social Anthropology I picked up a copy of David F. Lancy's *The Anthropology of Childhood: Cherubs, Chattel, Changelings* (2015). I could have read any of the popular "how to be parent/dad for dummies" books but I wanted to get a leg up on the other soon-to-be fathers and learn the secrets from other "cultures," so I could combine the best of all our world's parenthood teaching, to be truly worthy of the "World's Greatest Dad" mug that I some-day hope to attain (even if I have to buy it myself). Yes, it is the award that every father receives, similar to the participation trophies that are given to all of the children, regardless their performance, after a tournament or season's end.

As shown by Simmons, personhood, parenthood, and mother-hood are learned, not an innate nature or stable interior. It is here that I believe Lancy's work helps (though it is not the direct argu-ment of the book) to point out that we, as human beings, construct the very idea of "childhood," for it is not a given across all societies. For instance, I may see children playing and surmise that children love to play, and that much of childhood is play. I could argue then, that growing up is a process of moving from play to work. As that is the point of social media's use of #adulting, which distinguishes between our play and work as we grow into adulthood. Yet, as Mary Lorena Kenny's (2007) and Nancy Scheper-Hughes' (1992) eth-nographies of life in Brazil's favelas have shown, childhood and motherhood are not static identities around the world. In the case of Kenny, the age group we bracket in one context as set apart for play can be the same age when many children in Brazil become street kids, working to make a living for survival – for both themselves and their families. It is not a time for play but a time to adult. What we then also see is that it is the politics and modes of production as dictated by the elite class that structure and push members of a lower class to the periphery – which also defines their childhood. For Scheper-Hughes, motherhood is not purely a biological endeavor, rather it is shaped by economic and social conditions where mothers must choose between staying home to take care of their children (and possibly starving) or going out to find work while leaving a baby at home sometimes by itself. And, as Lancy notes, children can be characterized in a number of ways, including as commodities, laborers, or privileged overprotected consumers.

It is here that I find myself as a dad-to-be, about to dictate how a child should live – recognizing that I will be part of the process of constructing some form of identity for the child. For there is an "us" as parents and a "them" as children that becomes defined by the "us." In turn, the process says more about my social situatedness and myself than it does about the child. Even now, even before the child is born, parents (and thus the social environment in which parents exist) make many decisions on a child's behalf. As an example, consider the epic battle of pink and blue. Many people have asked me what the sex of our child will be (some slipping into a question of gender); after explaining that we won't be sharing that info, eyes light up stating "what a wonderful surprise that will be for everyone," and then after a short pause a second question arrives – "but what color clothing should we buy them?" Rather than explain immediately, I return with a question "what do you mean?" Their reply: "Well, if you have a boy, we can't buy them pink baby outfits, or even blue for girls." The irony of my question gets lost as I stand in front of them as a cis-gender straight male wearing a pink shirt – and yes, this has actually happened to me on multiple occasions. Suffice it to say that the "gender release parties" that have become popular as of late are not on our agenda.

While my own background in marketing makes the "pink girl" and "blue boy" historical narrative all that more amusing to me, it has become an important teaching moment for many educators when exploring the way we divide up the world via genders. A quick search of video-sharing sites such as YouTube provides a number of examples of how marketers and advertisers in the 1940s cemented a specific idea that boys needed one color (blue) and girls another (pink). Households with both female and male children needed to now buy gender-specific clothing (and toys) for each child – creating more sales for the company. It is not that varying clothing based on gender has not existed throughout history but, rather, that our idea of what are female- and male-appropriate colors has shifted. For gender is fluid and preformative (tip of the hat to Judith Butler

[1990]). While gender differentiation at first may seem like a solely symbolic structuring of society, economic reasoning is difficult to ignore in this case. There is nothing inherent that I am aware of in a child that identifies to me what color I should be dressing them in; instead, the discourse surrounding the colors that children wear tell us more about the people dictating what colors should be or should not be worn.

Where I arrive in this process is not that I am objectively right in my decisions that will shape a child (such as what colors they should wear) but rather that childhood is a flexible category. There is no common childhood, motherhood, or fatherhood across the planet – they are all fluid categories. And it is the awareness of this categorization and identity construction that I find helpful in examining what is at stake and for whom. Thus, childhood is not a "natural" or self-evident category and it is the analysis of those who are constructing these categories that should be our interest. It is the discourse surrounding childhood, motherhood, and fatherhood that now becomes the data.

And now I will return to building a crib and, in that very act, continue becoming a soon-to-be dad.

# References

Bayart, Jean-François (2005). *The Illusion of Cultural Identity.* Chicago: The University of Chicago Press.

Butler, Judith (1990). *Gender Trouble*. New York: Routledge.

Kenny, Mary Lorena (2007). *Hidden Heads of Households: Child Labor in Urban Northeast Brazil*. Toronto: University of Toronto Press.

McCutcheon, Russell T. (1997). *Manufacturing Religion: The Discourse on Sui Generis Religion and the Politics of Nostalgia*. Oxford and New York: Oxford University Press.

Scheper-Hughes, Nancy (1992). *Death Without Weeping: The Violence of Everyday Life in Brazil*. Berkeley and Los Angeles: University of California Press.

Jason W.M. Ellsworth, a doctoral student in Social Anthropology at Dalhousie University, Canada, is a lecturer in the Department of Religious Studies at the University of Prince Edward Island. His research interests include the anthropology of food, Buddhism in Canada, marketing and economy, transnationalism, and Orientalism.

# 21. Who Are You? I Am/Am Not a McCutcheonite

## Craig Martin

What's at stake in claiming an academic influence or identity, or in asserting another scholar's influence or identity? I've been accused of being a McCutcheonite before. What precisely is at stake in such an accusation? Why is it, for instance, an accusation rather than a form of praise? With this alleged identity claim, what is being accomplished?

On the one hand, clearly I'm a McCutcheonite in the banal sense that his work has influenced my own – and therefore I'm a McCutcheonite in the same sense that I'm also a Marxist, a Durkheimian, a Foucauldian, a Bourdieuean, a Derridean, a Butlerian, a (Wendy) Brownian, and so forth. Claiming an academic influence in this way is rather trite, however; it is just to suggest that some of the things that McCutcheon has written have theoretically informed my own writing projects. Such a claim doesn't assert a strict identity; while Durkheim's work has influenced my own work in a wide variety of ways, of course this by no means implies that I'm a slavish follower of Durkheim, incapable of my own thought or from whom I can never dissent. In fact, I have points of disagreement with all of the names above – there are many things Marx, Butler, and McCutcheon have said with which I am not in complete agreement. Presumably this is to be taken for granted – Lacan may have been a psychoanalyst but few would argue that he could not, by situating himself in Freud's intellectual tradition, depart from Freud's theory in any way. Rather, as almost everything Derrida wrote was at pains to demonstrate, claiming an influence is always and necessarily to signal indebtedness and departure simultaneously.

These things get complicated quickly with identities that carry a great deal of normative associations. For instance, while I can publicly say that there's much I dislike about Marcus Aurelius, Kant, or Gandhi, I'm much less likely to come away unscathed if I say I don't find anything of interest or use in the sayings of Jesus. Similarly, "Marxist" is a loaded term; in many contexts I could say I was a fan of Durkheim, Weber, Freud, or any other late-nineteenth- or early-twentieth-century figure, but if I say I find much to praise in the writings of Marx, I may be crossing a line, depending on the immediate audience.

But what about the *accusation* that I'm a McCutcheonite? I'm guessing that what's implied when others assert that I'm a McCutcheonite is not that his work has enjoyed some influence on my own, but rather that perhaps I'm an automaton incapable of thinking for myself – as if McCutcheon had an educational assembly line and I'm just another brick in the wall (cue up your memories of Pink Floyd's *The Wall* – "How can you have any pudding if you don't eat your meat?!"). In such cases I gather that the accusation is intended as damning. When I'm dismissed as a McCutcheonite, my work need not be read on its own – for presumably my work does not depart from McCutcheon's. On the contrary, whatever one assumes about McCutcheon (perhaps from having read only his first book, *Manufacturing Religion* [1997], or perhaps from one essay or one conference encounter, as if his work hasn't evolved over the almost twenty years he's been publishing) can be projected onto me as well. The messy work of actually reading what I have to say – and, for instance, comparing and contrasting it with the work of scholars who've influenced me – need not be undertaken. Perhaps all you need to know about Lacan is that he was a Freudian, and if you didn't like Freud then there's nothing new to learn from Lacan.

In addition, I gather that "McCutcheonite" additionally serves practically as an insult, a pejorative label like "Nazi" or "commie." McCutcheon's work has called into question a number of sacred cows in religious studies – the concepts of "religion," "faith," "experience," "authenticity," etc. – and I gather that dismissing someone as a McCutcheonite is a way of steering clear of such criticisms, perhaps in order to secure the status quo or continue going about scholarship in the usual way. (One wonders why anti-reductionists would reduce me to being a McCutcheonite if that is, in fact, a label I might contest.)

The scholars here at Culture on the Edge share a set of theoretical agendas, but – as with all social formations – there are necessarily differences suppressed for the sake of the shared interests. The presentation of us as homogeneous – either by us ourselves or by our opponents – is a mythmaking endeavor for the sake of some set of short-term or long-term goals. We are, however, no more homogeneous than all "women" or all "Muslims" are homogeneous. If that is the case, however, whose interests are served by the assertion that we're a homogeneous bunch? What do we gain by presenting ourselves as a united front? What do others gain by presenting us as a united front and then dismissing us out of hand?

I suppose I am/am not a McCutcheonite. I'll accept/contest the label depending on the context of the accusation.

Craig Martin is an Associate Professor of Religious Studies at St. Thomas Aquinas College. His research focuses on questions of theory and method in the study of religion, and his recent works include *A Critical Introduction to the Study of Religion* (2012) and *Capitalizing Religion: Ideology and the Opiate of the Bourgeoisie* (2014).

# 22. I Know You Are, but What Am I?

## Stacie Swain

> We are all at once writers, readers and protagonists of some eternal story; we fabricate our illusions, seek to decipher the symbols around us and see our efforts overstopped and cut short....
> (James E. Irby 1964: xxi)

In speaking of "writers, readers and protagonists," the quote above names multiple identities with which to describe oneself, positions from which to fabricate and decipher the external world and pursue interests within it. Instead of focusing upon the "writer," the "reader," or on "what is said to be an identity (a noun, naming a seemingly static item)," this volume seeks to examine these nouns or naming words as "the result of identity claims/acts and counterclaims/acts (verbs, signifying active processes)" (as phrased by McCutcheon in the introduction). Attention shifts from the "it" of an "identity" instead to the claims and acts that construct that "it." Instead of studying some*thing* called an "identity," we focus upon the words and actions of humans, or how we fabricate these seemingly stable descriptors in order to navigate and negotiate social interactions and situations. In this sense, we can instead ask when and why might one identify or be identified as an author, a reader, or a protagonist?

In the chapter preceding this one, Craig Martin, as both author and protagonist, identifies himself as an academic. An academic identity in the humanities or social sciences can be closely bound up with authorship due to contemporary degree requirements and the publishing expectations entailed by an academic career. Martin's position as a writer is thus in part due to his social context in addition, perhaps, to some internal quality made external. As a rhetorical question we might ask, does the "writer" precede the writing, or does the act of writing make one a writer?

Martin elucidates some of the claims and acts that go into fabricating his academic identity, specifically as he is/is not a "McCutcheonite" (a seemingly static noun). Martin's occasional identity as a McCutcheonite is fabricated by his own claims and by accusations from others – in other words, through verbs or active processes. Using Martin's chapter as data, and considering it alongside McCutcheon's introduction to this volume, and also drawing upon a few other examples of identity construction (such as the opening quote), I will expand upon Martin's piece before addressing his question: "What's at stake in claiming an academic influence or identity, or in asserting another scholar's influence or identity?"

The quote opening this chapter comes from the introduction to an edited collection of stories and other writings by Argentine author Jorge Luis Borges. The book came into my possession when I stumbled across a table of books being given away, set out in front of a university-affiliated bookstore. The books were free because they were too old to be donated to a library or school. Unable to resist (when a table of free books calls me into existence or [to borrow a technical term from Louis Althusser] "interpellates" me as a stereotypical graduate student, who loves books and getting things for free), I went home with backpack and arms full. Sections of the preface and introduction to the collected volume illustrate the construction of an identity through authorship – giving an indication that, for Borges, the answer to the question I posed earlier may have something to do with the act of writing creating the writer.

To begin with, and to refer back to the opening quote, we might understand how we fabricate our social milieu – things we call our "selves" and others' "selves," as paradoxical as the latter may seem – by imagining ourselves as participants in the production of a narrative, or in the context of life as literature (e.g., as a writer, a reader, a protagonist, and so on).[1] Simultaneously: one "writes" oneself and others through claims and assertions and, in turn, is "read" by (or interacts with) others, therefore influencing their own claims and assertions. One is thus fully situated within the context of one's own continually growing narrative *and* those of others, with all of the historicity and social contingency that these situations entail.

What then of an academic's narrative in particular, such as Martin's? What does an academic's work or interaction with other academics reveal? To begin with, consider that Martin refers to "influences." When he speaks of his own influences he lists McCutcheon among others, claiming that he is not only a McCutcheonite, but also potentially, "a Marxist, a Durkheimian, a Foucauldian, a Bourdieuean, a Derridean, a Butlerian, a (Wendy) Brownian, and so forth." In listing these influences, much like making a bibliography, Martin situates himself within the context of a particular discourse; he fabricates his academic identity by naming whom he reads and those he wants others to read his work in relation to.

This act of claiming or identifying an influence ought to draw our attention for several reasons. While citing the work of another (such as in my own first footnote) refers back to an earlier moment in time (when I read Calvino, for instance), the act of claiming that link while seeming to be about the past is itself firmly situated in the present. Citation refers to a statement in the past that is reconstructed to serve present purposes (e.g., my drawing the Italian author to your attention now). For example, take this tagline from the Google Scholar website's "About" page: "Stand on the shoulders of giants." In this case, cited scholars are identified as "giants" of their respective fields, whose foundational efforts enable the citing scholar to get a boost in their own work. For Martin, as for other academics, citation therefore works to further *Martin's* interests at *that* time (the time of writing) – not necessarily the interests of those whom he cites (who, of course, were citing yet others in the present moment

1 For an excellent example of a writer making a reader into a protagonist within fiction, see Italo Calvino's *If on a Winter's Night a Traveler* (trans. from Italian to English 1981).

of their writing, and so on, and so on…). One might even construct a so-called straw-man (or woman) argument, citing a scholar at length only to disagree with them.

In claiming or asserting an academic influence, one also contributes to the fabrication of the cited scholar's own identity (how readers read them, see them, situate their work, etc.) in addition to one's own. Turning again to literature, take for example, this description from the preface of the aforementioned Borges volume:

> Kafka *was* a direct precursor of Borges. *The Castle* might be by Borges, but he would have made it into a ten-page story, both out of lofty laziness and out of concern for perfection. As for Kafka's precursors, Borges's erudition finds pleasure in finding them in Zeno of Elea, Kierkegaard and Robert Browning. In each of these authors there is some Kafka, but if Kafka had not written, nobody would have been able to notice it – whence this very Borgesian paradox: 'Every writer creates his own precursors.'" (Maurois 1964: x–xi)

When Martin claims or cites an influence, he therefore contributes to the creation of his own precursors. This can be seen happening in academia, particularly through online citation tracking software. With Google Scholar, for example, or even some academic journals and library websites, citing a scholar creates a snowball effect. According to the "About" page, "Google Scholar aims to rank documents the way researchers do, weighing the full text of each document, where it was published, who it was written by, *as well as how often and how recently it has been cited in other scholarly literature*" (emphasis added). Citation is therefore one way in which present-day scholars recreate their own precursors and a version of the past, in addition to reconstructing (or deconstructing) previous ideas for their own purposes, let alone their own present place and thus identity. The more the citations, the taller (though not necessarily stronger) that giant's shoulders are to stand upon.

Moreover, in claiming an academic influence, one chooses which foundational thinkers will be read as authorizing one's own ideas. As already suggested, this very chapter provides an example.

I cite from literature (the Borges volume), McCutcheon's introduction, and Martin's chapter, before presenting my own ideas. In fact, McCutcheon authorizes *his* ideas by opening this volume with a quote from Jean-François Bayart. As Martin states, however, "claiming an influence is always and necessarily to signal indebtedness and departure simultaneously." Despite differences and due to similarities, we may be attributed with what Martin calls the "normative associations" of those we claim as influences. To use a different type of source as an example, what if on your Facebook page or Twitter account you were to repost an article sourced from the newspaper *The Wall Street Journal*, the tabloid *News of the World*, or the satirical online source *The Onion*? What if you were to cite one of the latter two in an academic paper? For each carries normative associations of credibility (or a lack thereof) contingent upon history and others' understanding of the source in question. The normative associations that others have about the source in question may affect their perceptions of your own qualities (i.e., credibility), contingently upon the context of the citation (i.e., on social media versus in academia).

Academics can be similarly self-conscious, not only in building credibility but also insofar as particular academic identities are assigned normative associations. For example, as Martin contends with respect to identification as a McCutcheonite, one may be expected or assumed to call into question core assumptions that some of those within the study of religion predicate their work upon and don't engage with. Using McCutcheon's work to authorize his own, claiming McCutcheon as an influence, or say, co-editing a volume with him, all contribute to the identification of Martin as a McCutcheonite. The associations (and benefits) Martin gains vary according to what the proper noun "McCutcheon" evokes for those doing the identifying, e.g., whether it's you or I (if, that is, you even have an opinion about this McCutcheon fellow's work or reputation). The fabrication of Martin's identity as a McCutcheonite relies upon the identifier, *and* the context in which that act of identification occurs. If Martin were to be identified as a McCutcheonite in a non-academic – in this case, a non-normative – context, the word may carry no associations for those present. As noted above, the fabrication of identities requires context(s) and social interaction.

Acts of identification, including using the term "McCutcheonite" as a pejorative, therefore always happen in relation to those around us. If we make the switch entertained at the start of this chapter and understand identities as socially constructed rather than as externalized individual essences, we can also examine how individual identity claims and assertions contribute to the formation and perpetuation of social groups. Groups exist at various levels of specificity, from academics in general to scholars in the study of religion, to, say, those focusing upon contemporary Neopaganism, ancient Judaism, or American religions. Affiliations that are based upon that which you study – e.g., a tradition, an ethnicity, a geographic location – assume some essential similarity within that category, or an "it" that erases differences.

Alternatively, a group may be identified according to what Martin calls a "theoretical agenda" – that is, by the approach that one takes, perhaps one similar to that of McCutcheon. Indeed, it's possible that Martin and others in the Culture on the Edge collective identify with each other *as* McCutcheonites or are identified in this manner by others who lump them together as McCutcheonites. Both methods of group formation entail what Martin describes as a "mythmaking endeavor," prioritizing homogeneity over heterogeneity for the sake of shared interests. Acts of identification therefore enable the navigation of social life, including within academic contexts, through fabrications of similarity and/or difference.

The introduction to this volume provides easily accessible data that illustrates a similarity/difference rhetoric. Every fabricated in-group has at least one, perhaps many, fabricated out-groups (that is, one cannot be this without simultaneously being not that). Take for example, McCutcheon's identification of those involved in authoring this book. There are:

1. The members of Culture on the Edge: at a variety of career stages, from tenure-track to full professors;
2. The respondents: at earlier stages of their careers, many doctoral students.

Here experience in academia is used to establish difference, while not only that all these writers are between the same covers but also that the contents cohere around a common theoretical agenda establishes similarity. If we read on, McCutcheon constructs another comparison and contrast. He marks as different,

3. "the number of scholars who still go about their work as if those things classed as religion were somehow a special case."

This implies that those within Culture on the Edge do *not* work under the assumption that religion is (or ever was) a special case. Indeed, McCutcheon goes on to state that there are,

4. "people to whom many of us [Culture on the Edge scholars] write." Namely, "a younger generation of scholars [see #2] who share many of our own frustrations with this [see #3] version of our field."

These claims are also acts of identification, only missing a proper noun to name those other groups in relation to Culture on the Edge. There are those scholars who think religion is special and work as such, and those who do not. And there are those younger scholars being written to, who are just beginning to construct their academic identities. Senior academics may be more or less likely to identify and interact with those within this younger generation depending upon their relation to them, the context of the interaction, and whether they have shared or competing interests.

More seemingly established identities are not necessarily more stable, for all that we might not be able to imagine Martin asserting the irrelevance of economics to the spiritual-but-not-religious trend, or McCutcheon expounding upon the values of confessional scholarship. Some academic identities *appear* more stable due to the temporal and material evidence of their fabrication relative to that of earlier career scholars. Were Martin or McCutcheon to undertake one of the projects above (projects not currently associated with their reputations), someone familiar with their work may not believe them based upon prior evidence to the contrary; that is, unless one wishes to believe that a conversion has taken place. Identity is to some extent in the hands and minds of others and results from prior social situations.

Claims and acts of identification, whether they be assertions or accusations, therefore fabricate the ways in which we appear to be an "I" and a "you," or a "this" and not a "that," contingent upon the context of the interaction. In a sense, the perfect response to any identity assertion or accusation is the potentially endless deferral of stable identity encapsulated in the childish retort: I know you are, but what am I? For every time that you make a claim about who *you* think *I* am, the act says something about *you*. At the same time, self-definition implicitly entails distinguishing oneself from others – a claim about who *I* think *you* are, says something about *me*.

As mentioned earlier, Martin asks, "What's at stake in claiming an academic influence or identity, or in asserting another scholar's influence or identity?" When it comes to academia, and particularly to any creative endeavor, in a sense our work *appears* to be the externalization of our ideas, or creativity. As I've argued, those ideas, though, are to some extent the result of prior and present social situations in which we find ourselves. Our work is therefore not the externalization of our identities, for identities are also ideas that we fabricate in the moment, in the doing, in the same way that we can simultaneously be writers, readers, and protagonists – or antagonists, sometimes. What is at stake then, is the extent to which we predicate who we think we are upon how (and through whom) we see ourselves to think and write, as individuals operating within a larger academic milieu. So, instead of coming before it, the individual might be constituted *by* that very milieu, by how and with whom we fabricate that which we afterwards call an "academic identity." This goes to show how situated, contingent, and contestable identities and identity claims are. What's at stake might therefore be an unsettling of unexamined or tightly-held assumptions about ourselves and others. So, who do you think you are? To end with a slightly modified version of the child's retort: if I'm rubber, and you're glue, your answer bounces off of me before it sticks to you.

# References

Bayart, Jean-François (2005 [1996]). *The Illusion of Cultural Identity.* Trans. Steven Rendall et al. Chicago: The University of Chicago Press.

Calvino, Italo (1981). *If on a Winter's Night a Traveler.* New York: Harcourt Brace Jovanovich.

Google Scholar. "About." https://scholar.google.ca/intl/en/scholar/about.html (accessed June 28, 2016).

Irby, James E. (1964). "Introduction." In Jorge Luis Borges, *Labyrinths; Selected Stories & Other Writings*, xv–xxiii. New York: New Directions.

Maurois, André (1964). "Preface." In Jorge Luis Borges, *Labyrinths; Selected Stories & Other Writings*, ix–xiv. Trans. Sherry Mangan. New York: New Directions.

Stacie Swain is a Master's student in Religious Studies at the University of Ottawa, Canada. She is interested in theory and method within and across disciplines and areas of study. Her current research examines the politics of the category of "religion" in reference to Indigenous peoples.

# 23. Who Are You? I'm Short (...and Cute)

## Leslie Dorrough Smith

Although "short and cute" aren't the first adjectives that I would usually choose to describe myself, they are among the more powerful identity categories that I deal with on a daily basis. I have always been one of the smallest of my peers, occupying the front row of group photos and living life with most of my kitchen cabinets just out of comfortable reach. Having said that, I am not unusually short – I am a little over 5'1", and I wear a women's size XS or S. In other words, while I would never claim that my appearance is representative of the majority of women in my culture, there are still plenty of others right around my size.

It might be tempting to think that we talk about each other's appearances simply because they're so visible and thus so seemingly available for conversation, in the same way that we might talk about how lovely a certain blue sky is on a clear day. Yet if there is anything that we know about beauty and appearance standards, it is that cultures construct them. That is, all cultures do not share a single, universal idea about what constitutes beauty or attractiveness, and all cultures manufacture and change these ideals as the trends, standards, and whims of that culture shift in response to different political and social arrangements. What this means, simply put, is that the criteria that constitute beauty and attractiveness are interesting barometers of the power relationships that exist in a society.

So despite the fact that my appearance is not particularly remarkable in that respect, it still crops up as a frequent theme in my interactions with others. Why? My sense is that this has something to do with the dynamics of gendered, heteronormative power and the identity markers upon which it depends.

Let's consider how we use the word "cute," particularly as we apply it to women. While "cute" may seem to be nothing more than a compliment, it is a term with its own set of baggage. It is probably a hopeless task to disentangle the differences in meaning that are deployed in the words "cute" and "beautiful," but I will go out on a limb and briefly suggest that while both might indicate that the bearer meets a particular aesthetic standard, "cute" is often a subset lower than "beautiful" when one is attempting to gauge attractiveness. The blunting of aesthetic appeal implicit in "cuteness" versus "beauty" may be more of a statement about one's perceived power, for "cute" is also associated with overt infantilizing tones – with inherent weakness, innocence, delicacy, or vulnerability (think how often we describe children and baby animals using the term). This is why if a woman, in particular, is taller or larger, the term "cute" tends to be used less often to describe her, for part of the aesthetic appeal behind cuteness is that it involves a certain presumed vulnerability of size.

In effect, "cute" can operate as the linguistic moment when what is normally considered a weakness transforms into female desirability. You may be familiar with feminist scholar Catherine MacKinnon's observation that, in heteronormative cultures, female standards of beauty are determined largely by men, and thus what is deemed attractive for women is usually a reflection of what maintains male empowerment, both physical and ideological.[1] This is, I suspect, why the ever present "Sexy Schoolgirl" Halloween costume returns year after year to the retail store shelves, despite our culture's general revulsion for pedophilia. The schoolgirl becomes sexy precisely because she is childlike, innocent, and vulnerable at the same time that she is sexually available. In other words, her perceived powerlessness is an important piece of her desirability.

As such, those of us who bear the label may agree that "short and cute" frequently operates as a something of a dismissal couched

1 This is one of the larger theses of MacKinnon 1989.

in a compliment. For instance, the following are things that have happened to me, sometimes with regularity, that are a direct result of my appearance:

I find that strangers in social situations often touch me more than others. My husband very frequently attends social events for work, and I am usually surrounded at these events by taller, often older, men who know my husband but not me. Throughout these events I am hugged and air-kissed (which is far more physical than it sounds!) by men I don't know with a frequency that I do not see women taller or larger than me experiencing. (Although this is clearly anecdotal data, after years and years of attending these events, a clear pattern has emerged.) In addition to the physical contact, I am told with astonishing regularity that I remind someone of their daughter, granddaughter, etc.

On a number of different occasions, I have had otherwise well-meaning teachers, professors, and even senior colleagues quote that line from Shakespeare's *A Midsummer Night's Dream* ("Though she be but little, she is fierce!") in moments where we were talking about something entirely divorced from my appearance or English literature. While I used to take this as a sort of funny compliment, it has only recently occurred to me how odd it would be to use famous literature to invoke the physical characteristics of my conversation partner in the middle of a discussion on grading rubrics.

I am often told by people who have read my scholarship that, when they meet me in person, they are surprised by my height, with most presuming that I should be taller than I am. Since I can only presume that these people are sincere in their flattery of my work, I think it is also safe to presume that their expectations of my body size are grounded in the subliminal symbolism that equates formidability with a taller or larger physical presence.

And then there is the ongoing battle that I face at certain grocery stores, where I not infrequently have the folks bagging the groceries go to great lengths to ensure that my bags are not overfilled (interestingly, when my husband and I are together, this rarely happens). On one particularly noteworthy occasion when I was shopping alone, the man bagging the groceries wanted me to take the time to physically attempt to lift each bag and to mimic hoisting it into my trunk to gauge whether I could handle it. This could have been interpreted as overzealous courtesy, except that I had just told him I did not have time to do this and that I was plenty strong. He insisted I try, because, in his words, it was important to him that he "treat me like a lady."

While I would not suggest that my experiences are universal, I am sure I am not the only "short and cute" woman who has experienced sexism through this particular labeling mechanism. It is commonplace in our culture to sidestep serious consideration of body standards by insisting that we are all beautiful in our own way, and yet claiming such things only reinforces the centrality of this category "beauty" without ever asking who benefits from its deployment. The primary question that should engage scholars of identity, then, is how terms like "short and cute" are used to create differentiations that impact all realms of social life. In this sense, much like a tee shirt that one of my children has (which is emblazoned with the statement "I'm not short! I'm fun-sized!"), "short and cute" talk is not mindless banter, but is a recuperation of longstanding – if still, to most, relatively invisible – attitudes towards gender and power that masquerade as flattery.

# Reference

MacKinnon, Catharine (1989). *Towards a Feminist Theory of the State.* Cambridge, MA: Harvard University Press.

Leslie Dorrough Smith is Associate Professor of Religious Studies and Director of the Women's and Gender Studies program at Avila University. Her research focuses on the impact of religious rhetoric on attitudes and policy towards sex, gender, and reproduction in the United States. She is the author of *Righteous Rhetoric: Sex, Speech, and the Politics of Concerned Women for America* (2014).

# 24. I'm "Irish," Torontonian, ...French?

**Matthew Sheedy**

For as long as I can remember my father has been teased by family and close friends for his tendency to go on a little long with stories, to which he always replies, in a playful-yet-slightly-defensive tone, "Oh, leave me alone. I'm Irish." I never thought much of this until my early twenties when I began to question just what exactly was Irish about us? Like my father, I was born and raised in Toronto, Ontario, long after the deaths of my paternal great-grandparents who migrated from the West coast of Ireland. Growing up we had no family from the old country with whom we were in contact, and any talk of "Irish-ness" was vague and without the usual markers of identity, such as accent, love of soccer/football/hurling, or a discernible tradition of storytelling to lend it an air of "authenticity."

I took up this vague "Irish" identity with full force in my teens, though looking back it seems that this was largely motivated by a desire to gain social capital with two of my closest friends and their families who came directly from Ireland, accents and all. After my first trip to Ireland at the age of twenty, I began to think that my Irish-ness was more aspirational than anything else and, apart from the thrill of seeing my family name emblazoned on a storefront window – Sheedy's Pub – I realized that I didn't have all that much in common with this imagined identity. In the years that followed, I have lived in Santiago, Chile; St. John's, Newfoundland; and, Winnipeg, Manitoba, and find myself no longer able to think of my identity as separate from the influence of the people that I meet in the places that I inhabit.

Jean-François Bayart touches on one aspect of these shifting acts of identification when he writes:

> For example, someone from Saint-Malo will define himself as a resident of that town when dealing with someone from Rennes, as a Breton when dealing with someone from Paris, as French when dealing with someone from Germany, as a European when dealing with an American...as Catholic when dealing with a Protestant.... (2005: 92)

In a similar vein, I have often described myself as being "from the Avenue and Wilson area" when in Toronto (Avenue and Lawrence is more accurate, but has bourgeois connotations, so I avoid it), as "Torontonian" when outside of the city but still inside Canada, as "Canadian" when travelling abroad (with the proviso that I'm originally from Toronto), and as a "settler" of mostly Irish decent (not British!) when talking to Indigenous friends in Winnipeg, where I now live. Depending on who is asking and what I gage their politics to be, I might also describe myself as a non-theist, a "perennial agnostic," or a heretic – the latter term being reserved for Catholics whom I know to have a sense of humor (or if I'm just feeling punchy). Functionally, I may also be described as an atheist, though I avoid this personal marker of identity due to its current "rationalist" valence in many Euro-Western societies (thanks Richard Dawkins!). In all cases, these various acts of identification will provoke different responses in people that, in turn, will influence my future choices of self-description based on what I think works best in any given situation.

Apart from certain empirical descriptions such as one's status of citizenship, which is factually true by convention of law (e.g., I hold a passport from country X), acts of identification based on ethnicity or religion are fluid constructions that depend upon things like shifting perceptions of ourselves over time, our geographical location, the influence and perceived judgments of others, and, not least, the amount of social capital that we hold in a particular social field. This includes cultural and economic status, which may cause us to distinguish, emphasize, or downplay certain aspects of our identity over others due to a perceived social advantage among different groups. For example, to identify myself as Canadian is typically looked upon rather favorably by my American friends, though not among some of my First Nations friends who define themselves in opposition to the Canadian state.

In her essay, "Who Are You? I'm Short (...and Cute)," Leslie Dorrough Smith recalls several instances when she has been referred to as "cute" by strangers, and argues that this seemingly innocent description works to reinforce the idea that smaller-statured adult women are vulnerable and in need of (male) protection. In this way, the term cute "masquerade[s] as flattery" while maintaining a form of "gendered, hetero-normative power." Even when these assumptions appear to be subverted, as when a smaller-statured woman is labeled as "feisty" or "fierce," such modifiers do not overturn the association with vulnerability or weakness so much as they suggest an exception to a general rule (and perhaps a warning to stay away!).

Dorrough Smith's observations provide a useful instance of how certain qualities or descriptions about people that we tend to assume are complimentary are often loaded with ideological baggage, and work to naturalize ideas about (in this case) women, while reinforcing behaviors toward them in subtle ways. I can find nothing to disagree with in Dorrough Smith's piece, as she nicely captures the ambiguities and malleability of power structures and their ability to shape-shift as more overt stereotypes become less socially acceptable. Taking her observations a few steps further, we might also ask how the label "cute" relates to Dorrough Smith's own social position, including how it is affected or might change in different environments, or in relation to other variables like age, race, socio-economic class, religious identity, and so forth.

As a well-educated, white, cis-gendered male in his mid-thirties living in Canada in 2016 (all fluid identity markers in themselves), I (currently) have the advantage of an outward appearance that goes largely "unmarked," in the sense that I am not typically labeled as "Other" nor subject to discrimination (unlike most women). Consequently, I feel no need to either distance myself from or embrace a particular ethnic, gendered, or cultural identity as an act of positive self-assertion or resistance (unlike many who are labelled "minorities"). As the comedian Louis C.K. once quipped, "I'm a white man, you can't even hurt my feelings!" Such forms of unearned privilege are marked not only by an absence of discrimination, but also through the presence of cultural productions that reflect the tastes and preferences or "habitus" of "majority" groups. In a North American context, these cultural productions (e.g., in film, in advertising, etc.) tend to reproduce the interests of white, straight, middle-to-upper-class, cis-gendered men, which has the effect of making particular and contingent identities seem like a natural reflection of who "we" are. One example of such acts of identification (and their malleability) can be seen in a fairly recent beer commercial that attempts to define what it means to be "Canadian."

In 2013, the Molson brewing company released an ad entitled "The Canadians,"[1] which generated over one million hits in under a week. The ad follows conversations between locals in Berlin, Dublin, Cape Town, Tokyo, and "somewhere in the Australia," all of whom share in common an encounter with a Canadian in a bar the previous evening. Here are a few of their exchanges:

> In Cape Town, a young women remarks to her friend, "He goes into the bar with a tree trunk…, the next thing I know he put the tree trunk over his head."

> In Berlin, a women muses to her partner, "[He was] kind of crazy in a good way. He was funnier than you, Claus."

> In Dublin, another young women quips to a friend, "She sang badly, but everyone loved her. They couldn't stop cheering for her."

After the telling of these various tales, it is revealed (and in each case to the surprise of the listener) that these fun-loving, endearing, and all-too-eccentric characters are Canadian. The remainder of the

---

1 You can find the video at https://vimeo.com/64339497 (accessed July 5, 2016).

ad presents a montage meant to illustrate these particular qualities, with scenes of people sliding through mud, jumping in water with their clothes on, a woman crowd-surfing in a canoe at a concert and, just for good measure, two young (white) women on the verge of kissing underwater in a swimming pool – the latter being a rather telling instance of "gendered hetero-normative power" intended to appeal to a target male demographic of beer drinkers. In all of these examples, it is not clear what markers of cultural identity are being upheld, or what, precisely, is so "Canadian" about them.

This commercial got me thinking about an earlier, widely popular Molson commercial from 2000, that offers a much more concrete attempt to define markers of national identity. Entitled, "I am Canadian: The Rant,"[2] the ad opens with a man who looks to be in his early thirties cautiously walking out on stage to a room full of Americans. As he begins his rant, which ends in a loud crescendo of jingoistic fervor with the trademark slogan, "I am Canadian," he recounts a number of attributes of "Canadianness," at first negative and then positive:

> I'm not a lumberjack or a fur trader and I don't live in an igloo or eat blubber or own a dogsled.... I speak English and French, not American.

> I can proudly sew my country's flag on my backpack.

> I believe in peacekeeping not policing, diversity not assimilation.

> Canada is the second largest landmass, the first nation of hockey and the best part of North America.

One thing to note here, especially when compared with the more recent Molson ad, is how most of these positive attributes of "Canadianness," defined in opposition to "America," have all but

2 Posted at https://www.youtube.com/watch?v=WMxGVfk09IU (accessed July 4, 2016).

lost their former currency in the social imagination. Given recent political developments – like Canada's role in the "war on terror" and its shift away from peacekeeping as a dominant mode of foreign policy, its global pariah status on environmental issues under the government of Stephen Harper (2006–15),[3] and recent controversies surrounding attempts to ban the veil worn by Muslim women in the public service in Quebec in 2013 – the myth of a peaceful, diversity-loving nation with a great reputation abroad doesn't seem to hold the same currency it once did.

Paying attention to things like changing social and economic policies may help to explain the shift in Molson's patriotic ad campaigns from 2000 to 2013, where myth-making in the interest of national identity morphed from certain concrete markers of "Canadianness" that were assumed to be obvious toward a rather vague and diffuse form of liberal individualism, where affability and eccentricity stand in for a much wider range of sensibilities – that is, if you're young, drink beer, are (mostly) white, can afford to travel and, apparently, like to do things in mud and water.

While all identities are constructed, they are far from arbitrary and do have significant social effects, especially for those who are classified by dominant groups in ways that enable the maintenance of social hierarchies. Two such examples can be seen with the US professional baseball team, the Cleveland Indians, and the US professional football team, the Washington Redskins. In the first instance, a symbol for Indigenous culture is being appropriated by non-Indigenous people, and has the effect of naturalizing a term (Indian) that is not commonly accepted by those people it identifies. In the case of "Redskins," it has recently been discussed in some media that this term has ties to the violent act of scalping by European settlers, which has provoked considerable backlash and demands to change the team's name. To be sure, the meaning of these terms has shifted over time and, in the case of "Indian," it is often taken up by Indigenous people in North America themselves

---

3  For example, see: http://www.huffingtonpost.ca/2012/12/05/canada-worst-climate-policy_n_2246238.html (accessed July 1, 2016).

to identify fellow insiders, giving a positive valance to a once negative attribution. Paying attention to such strategies of identification
– who is doing the labeling and to what end – can tell us a lot about
how they function within different social economies, and shifts
attention away from the conceit that identities exist as stable entities
over time toward a recognition that they are always contingent upon
things like self interest or one's position in a social hierarchy.

## Postscript

While reading over this reply to Leslie Dorrough Smith, I realize
that it is itself an act of identification. The selection of some aspects
of my identity over others reveals a privileged place within my own
social world, as I am relatively free to define myself without the
imposition of being "marked" by others. I also realize that I have
neglected to mention my maternal grandfather's French Canadian
heritage (from which I had distanced myself in my youth) revealing
a process of identification by omission that I have unconsciously
internalized and continue to resist to this day. Perhaps if I find
myself living in Quebec or in France at some point in the future, I
may find a reason to reimagine my identity once again....

## Reference

Bayart, Jean-François (2005 [1996]). *The Illusion of Cultural Identity*.
Trans. Steven Rendall et al. Chicago: The University of Chicago Press.

Matthew Sheedy received his PhD in Religious Studies at the University of
Manitoba (2015), Winnipeg, and is co-editor of the *Bulletin for the Study
of Religion* blog and *Religion Compass*. His research interests include
critical social theory, theories of secularism, as well as representations of
Christianity, Islam, and Native traditions in popular and political culture.

# Afterword: Express Yourself

## Russell T. McCutcheon

"For the apparel oft proclaims the man…"
– Polonius (*Hamlet*, Act 1, Scene 3)

If you have worked through the preceding chapters, then by now you may have arrived here either thoroughly or partially persuaded that the commonsense model that we normally use to talk about identity needs to be rethought – at least when we're trying *to study* this thing called identity. For when we're just talking about our identity, i.e., whether we're crossing a border and producing our passport or knee-deep in making and contesting any number of other identity claims in day-to-day life (like debating who's *really* a Muslim or which gender someone *really is* – to name just two among countless sites in the news these days), then what I'll call the commonsense model likely serves us well, inasmuch as it assumes (as noted in the introduction and across a variety of the chapters) the existence of some permanent, inner quality that is, in some secondary step, thrown outward into the world where it is seen and read (and, we might feel, sometimes misread) by others. But *studying* identity – that is, talking about identity-talk itself and thereby closely examining the process by which we come to think that each of us just naturally possesses (or, on second thought, might we say *is possessed by*?) some set of unchanging traits or dispositions – requires a shift in our approach, to try to remove ourselves from the contest in order to scrutinize it; it is a shift that depends upon a rigorous self-consciousness concerning the ease of slipping in and out of the commonsense model even when we claim to be doing something different, something, for lack of a better word, *scholarly*.

So, as I said above, even if you think that the forgoing chapters have persuaded you, it might not hurt to offer one final, extended meditation on the shift that this book's authors all explore – especially given the temptation to fall back into thinking that identities simply lurk inside us and, at some later time, are merely expressed in public (not unlike a movie projected from a source onto a screen). But given that some readers might *not* be persuaded at all after reading all that came up to this point, this is also the last opportunity to suggest that something might be gained by rethinking how each of us positions ourselves – a rethinking that may have us entertaining that we are instead *positioned by others* – in order to be understood as, as we say, having an identity.

So, to start off, consider this one example: a good friend, some years ago, told me the story of his two slightly younger brothers debating among themselves who was a truer example of a western Canadian. For while one brother had stayed out west, for his career and with his family, the other had found a life in the east, in Toronto (the largest city in Canada, and the self-proclaimed business center of the nation – making it somewhat disliked by some who live elsewhere in the country). With one basically accusing the other of having sold out by heading east, the brothers happily jousted with each other, trying to establish their own legitimacy as westerners. "Just the other day, in fact, I had pasta for dinner!" the one retorted, as part of this negotiation, presumably to demonstrate his continued working-class sensibilities despite his home in the big city; "Aha!" the other replied, as if scoring a point, adding: "When we were kids you would have called it *macaroni!*"

It might be useful for readers to keep this anecdote in mind, as if overhearing it while we were doing fieldwork among what we, the observers, find to be a strange and thus curious group of people involved in some sort of ritual performance; for here, I would argue, we see an example of identification in action – perhaps a simple example, yes, maybe even a fun one, but also one which, I'd further argue, sheds light on basic principles at work whenever we find identification taking place or an identity being claimed.

So what first strikes me as interesting in this case is that, prior to being questioned on his authenticity as a westerner, and thus the continued legitimacy of his place (within the family, within the province, etc.), the slightly older, pasta-eating brother was probably not thinking much about his identity – whether he had one, much less what it was or if it had changed over time. Until the moment of a challenge – such as a younger sibling poking you with an unanticipated query that calls something into question – I presume that we each simply go about our lives in a rather un-reflective manner. While we of course are able to engage in rigorous acts of self-examination, those moments likely don't come naturally to us, spontaneously and of their own accord; we all know the words to a national anthem yet, while singing them, we usually are not thinking about how we were taught them, and by whom, or the earliest occasion when we first sang what were then unfamiliar words to an unfamiliar tune, let alone mulling over the social implications of knowing that we are in a group of people all engaged in like behaviors (e.g., singing the same song, facing the same direction, with hands over hearts, perhaps). Instead, moments of self-reflection probably result from a social situation, an interaction, such as the one described above, in which a claim of identity is made in the midst of, and thus in reply to, a contest – in fact, we might go so far as to suggest that claims of identity result from the contest itself. For, prior to the challenge, I'd guess that this brother wasn't much concerned with what he'd eaten the other day, and what it might signify about who he was – or, better put, who he could be considered to be in his brother's eyes. However, as a result of the challenge, and because his assumed place was suddenly in question, an effort was made to use whatever was at hand – such as a memory of eating a dinner that could function as an emblem of a certain way of being in the world – to create the impression of a bond where, at least to his younger sibling, none was claimed to exist.

So what we have here, at least if we approach the topic in this manner, is identity not as the expression of a stable, inner feeling but, instead, as something conjured up in the social moment of a very public challenge – a counter-claim specifically designed to answer the need of a particular occasion. Change the occasion and it's likely that the reply would vary as well – suggesting to us that, when viewed from this angle, identity is far more fluid and situationally-specific, even tactical, than we might at first think. If so, then employing the commonsense model (the one that says we each just have identities lurking somewhere on the inside) helps us little to study what was taking place when those two brothers arm-wrestled over who had sold out and who had remained faithful; as I said above, a shift is needed, if we're intent on thinking critically about this thing we so easily just call identity.

And the key to this rethinking is, I think, our re-examination of a word often used when conversations turn toward this topic of identity – in fact, I've already used it a few times above. The word is: *express*.

While the modern usage of language is certainly not dictated by earlier uses, sometimes there's something to be learned by determining the source for our words. Sharing a history with the Italian word *espresso* – in which hot water is forced through the tightly packed coffee grounds – the common English word "express" is, like so much of our language, usually traced back to Latin: combining the prefix *ex-* (meaning from out of, and even upward) with the term for pushing or pressing (Latin: *pressare*) results in a word that we commonly employ today to name both a process of movement as well as meaning-making – a word so familiar to us that, when using the term, we likely don't give its connotations a second thought. For we are so used to talking about "expressing ourselves" or judging some choice of words as an "odd expression," that our use of language in such cases surely strikes us as insignificant. But bearing in mind from where these terms derive (which requires us to see language and even meaning-making itself as historical and thus changeable – the first step in rethinking identity as being just as malleable, perhaps) invites us to scrutinize just what might be going on when we often and so casually understand communication to be a process whereby something is pushed from the inside out.

To do this sort of re-examination we could use another example – something else to inspect and consider from a variety of vantage points, hoping to learn something that we had not previously understood when we approached it with the traditional understanding of how identity is an inside-out projection. So, consider the appropriately titled 1970 funk hit, "Express Yourself," by Charles Wright & the Watts 103rd Street Rhythm Band. (Unfamiliar with it? Well, you should give it a listen....) Reaching number three on the R&B charts, the song with the memorable beat opens as follows:

> Express Yourself
> Express Yourself
> You don't never need help
> From nobody else
> All you got to do now
> Express Yourself
> Whatever you do (Uh)
> Do it good (Uh)
> Whatever you do (do do Lord Lord)
> Do it good.
> All right...

Even in just the opening lines the lyrics make plain that "you don't never need help, from nobody else," since expressing yourself – putting your self forward, pushing it out into the world from its usual interior homes – is an individual act if ever there was one. For if the thing being pressed outward is one's very identity – one's truest, most authentic self, the private quality that (as the Latin precursor of the very word identity suggests), is, was, and will be uniform and thus always the same – then how could anyone even assist in such act? Now, if our word "express" derives from earlier terms that meant not only to press outward but, thereby, also to represent something (as in a copy, a facsimile, thereby making something present once again, on the outside and not just on the inside, over and over again), and, further, if, as I just suggested, our word "identity" comes from the Latin for the quality of being the same, then we see here, in this one funk song, the commonplace or folk notion that we all walk around with as we each interact with one another in the world: that we each possess a unique, stable, internal quality that distinguishes each of us from everyone else, copies of which we each project outward into the world around us; while this identity may overlap to varying degrees with those of others (i.e., we do share some traits, of course, since some of us are vegetarians or some of us are western Canadians…), your specific blend of characteristics is not only truly and uniquely your own but it is assumed to endure over time (consider the example of an elderly person pointing to a old photograph of a child and saying "That's me."). And, at least according to this model, the only way for us to experience anyone else's true self is for each of us to push it outward, to manifest it (as a previous generation of scholars might have put it) in the world, by means of symbols, style of dress (as suggested by that quote from Shakespeare that opened this Afterword), or, as we saw a little earlier, what we ate for dinner the other evening. "Whatever you do, do it good," the singer says, in order to "express yourself."

But this widely accepted model – and, like I said, it is a model that we each use throughout our lives, at countless moments – starts to crumble a bit when we look at it a little more closely (as each of the authors in this volume did). Case in point: much like the older brother replying to the challenge, without the singer's admonition, would each of us be spontaneously expressing ourselves (whatever that may or may not mean)? It may seem a minor point, but, much like the younger brother's challenge, the voice of the singer, singing what the lyricist wrote, can't be overlooked in all this; for listening to a song that advocates a highly individual act – after all, "You don't never need help, from nobody else…" – is a curiously contradictory moment, if you think about it; for songs (like all of culture, one could argue) are themselves remnants of prior social moments. To rephrase the point, this song, like all others, did not spring from the ground all on its own and does not exist in the private recesses of someone's mind. Instead, it was written by people, in a particular time and a place, and in this case in English – a language none of the writers or singers invented on their own – and put to a tune with melodies and a chorus – the strict structure of a pop hit was hardly their invention either. What's more, it is part of global capitalism – for there's a record company, after all, understandably seeking to make a profit from the buying and selling of music and there's also that artist likely hoping for royalties (though, in the early days of pop music, artists often lacked ownership over their music). Apart from appreciating it for having what once might have been called "a funky groove," the song can also be understood as a social, political, economic, etc., artifact, that – and here we should become rather curious – somehow posits the existence of a non-social, non-political, non-economic, etc., zone or moment buried somewhere deep in its listeners – their pre-expressed selves, as it were – for whose public expression the song advocates.

What's so interesting, then, is that something that, by definition, is said to *defy* public perception (and thus elude detection by others) is presumed to come into public existence *only because other people, in public, were calling for it*. (Aside: in many versions of the lyrics there's an exclamation mark after "express yourself," implying that it is an imperative statement, i.e., a command, and not just an idle request or mere suggestion.) To rephrase: If you truly "don't never need help, from nobody else" then why write and sing this song, let alone listen to it or allow it to shape your behavior (as in being inspired by it)? So here we have a classic example of a contradiction (the double negative of the lyric might be an ironic clue that something's up) – the message of the song is undermined by that which conveys the message (i.e., the song itself); for if the message was correct then there'd be no reason to advocate, as the singer does, and thus the song would not even exist. For a song such as this would then probably be seen as utterly trivial, inasmuch as it contains a completely unnecessary message. Or, to put it in terms we associate with 1960s media analysis (and the work of someone like the late Marshall McLuhan, who was among those who early on argued that content was always a function of context and didn't simply pre-exist it): the existence of the medium (that is, the song itself) undermines, or opposes, its own message concerning the irrelevance of public input.

Should our analysis be influenced by a long tradition of social theory that traces its roots to the writings of Karl Marx, this constitutes an example of how social institutions are inevitably established on contradictions – institutions whose smooth functioning depends upon such contradictions going undetected. As but one example, consider the fact that many of us commonly claim to live in a free country (as the US national anthem finishes, "… the land of the free and the home of the brave"), yet it is not difficult at all to quickly find a large number of constraints on our behavior (e.g., you don't yell "Fire!" in a crowded movie theater); in fact, one's contentment (even pride) with living in the US likely depends, to varying degrees, on us *not worrying too much* about how this claim is called into question by such mundane examples as speed limits, rules of etiquette, or libel laws. To press further, perhaps "free" or our sense of "freedom" names the zone created by those laws and those limits – that is, if we take the parameters set by such things as speed limits for granted (that is, accepting that you can get a ticket for going either too slow or too fast), thereby granting the government the right to determine the limits for how fast we can drive our cars (after all, we don't have autobahns, as they do in Germany, where there are sometimes no speed limits), then "freedom" names operations within that domain, within those limits, inasmuch as we can decide to drive, let's say, 50 miles per hour in a 65 limit zone, or 51 miles per hour, or 52, and so on and so on. Thus we *feel* free. But this rather more constrained, delimited, and controlled notion of freedom is likely not what the US national anthem is about, at least to the people who are singing it – suggesting again that problematizing, and thereby making curious, our commonsense models is among the things that scholarship can do.

Considering how a larger structure can make possible certain meanings or specific sorts of experiences starts to bring us back to making a shift in how we understand identity to work – or, better put, how the always ongoing process of identity formation takes place. For if, as I've just argued, freedom is not some utterly unfettered and unregulated state in which we can do anything we want, but, instead, is the place we inhabit that was created by the intersection of a variety of rules and systems (comprising a structure that, because of our familiarity with it, we see to be so normal as to let it go unnoticed, allowing us to *feel* unencumbered despite always operating within limits that would likely be pretty apparent to those who are unfamiliar with them), then perhaps this thing that we each call identity may also *not* be an inner, eternal quality only later projected or expressed outward but, instead, *might be a sense that we each gain about ourselves when – like the brother described above – we are placed within specific sorts of situations and specific sorts of relationship to others who happen to be around us*. Consider the earlier example of the song and someone hearing it for the first time, back in 1970; it was at a time when long-established social and political structures in the US were coming under new and, at times, rigorous scrutiny and even critique. The situation of the song (its context) might therefore be important to keep in mind if we're interested in studying its content; so we can't forget about what was then a growing US war in Vietnam, controversy and political upheaval at home, race relations strained and the Civil Rights movement in full swing, the feminist movement gaining in speed, assassinations of leaders just two years earlier (I'm speaking here of Martin Luther King and Bobby Kennedy, of course) ...; all can be seen to have contributed to a drastic and, at the time of the song, ongoing change in what might have seemed to some as once established and secure social relations (and thus the identities that result). And so, with this changing structure, and its different limits, came new opportunities to experiment with who "we" each were, i.e., who others perceived us to be, with whom we interacted and how. And thus, contrary to the commonsense model, and contrary to how we at first read that song, we can now entertain that identity may instead be how we respond (and are seen by others to respond) to the situations in which we find ourselves.

As but one more quick example, consider how illegitimate I (and perhaps you as well?) recall feeling when I first started high school or even university, or when I got my first job as a professor – not knowing the layout of the school, not knowing the habits, not knowing others and thus my place among them, etc. But, with increased familiarity, with newly established friendships and learning the ropes, as they once said, I eventually came to see myself as being "in high school," or as being "a university student" or "a professor." It felt similarly awkward to talk about "my girlfriend," then "my fiancée," and finally "my wife" – to think through that I was now someone's boyfriend, fiancé, husband (words that all mark changed social relations). Like the old joke when a fellow is greeted by the title Mr, and the guy assumes they're talking about his father – the humor trades on the out-of-place feeling one has when treated as one presumes others ought to be treated, as in when a server in a restaurant who might not be much younger than you calls you Ma'am. Older people certainly become accustomed to this (and take it to be a mark of deference on the part of the person in the socially inferior position), to such an extent that *not* calling them Ma'am or Sir might jar them somewhat; but early on the title contradicts the identity one has adopted – or the one that has been forced upon you by others, which is undermined by the one now presented by way of the server addressing you with a more formal title.

To press the point that environmental conditions may actually create identities rather than just being the blank canvas onto which our inner worlds are projected, consider an interview, broadcast on National Public Radio in the US in the summer of 2016,[1] just a couple months after the majority of British voters signaled their interest to leave the European Union; given the EU's so-called "open borders" policy for member states (allowing the free movement of their citizens), Great Britain's exit would have profound implications for immigration policy in the country as well as for current non-nationals living and working there. As the radio report told it:

> Twenty-two-year-old Raquel Gallego, who was sitting in Trafalgar Square not long ago, came from southern Spain to become an *au pair*. "In Spain there are no jobs and little opportunity, and I always liked London and England so it was

1 Find the full story here: http://www.npr.org/sections/parallels/2016/07/27/487577881/after-brexit-uncertainty-over-status-of-eu-workers-living-in-u-k (accessed July 27, 2016).

just the moment to do it," she says. Gallego says she wants to settle in London and work with disabled children. Right now she can stay as long as she wants. But many people in Britain believe immigration is dragging down wages, especially for low-skilled work, and true or not those fears played a part in June's Brexit vote. The vote has left the status of foreign workers uncertain. Gallego's friend, Sanne Krukkert, who's from the Netherlands, says a lot of long-time immigrants she knows are considering leaving Britain. "I know a lot of people they are not feeling English anymore, and they're like for the first time ever I feel like I'm from a different country and I'm not from here anymore," Krukkert says.

It's that last quotation from Sanne Krukkert that might now catch our attention: the feeling of Englishness that some immigrants apparently had developed, having lived much of their lives in England and thus having become accustomed to being enveloped by an English world (everything from clothing, vocabulary, and accents to food, the weather, and landscapes), has suddenly been undermined by the changing social, political, and economic conditions. (And it's clear from listening to other interviews conducted among those voting to leave the EU that the presence of immigrants there, and the authority the EU exercised over daily life there, had contributed to the conditions that led to many even longer-time residents feeling that they were losing their own distinctiveness as English! So it cuts both ways.) Of course, as some might argue, one could counter that, as immigrants, they had *inappropriately* thought that they were English and only now was their error apparent to them. (For, as this position would maintain, they're not English at all but actually Spanish or Dutch.) After all, as someone adopting this position might continue, they never possessed any essentially English identity. Countering such an assertion is not all that difficult, however, since it could be easily argued that *everyone comes from someplace else and thus that there are no such things in the world as, in this one example, essentially English traits*. Case in point: while I could discuss my own sense of being Canadian despite ancestors from Scotland, Ireland, and France (and who knows where else), consider the far more loaded example of Queen Elizabeth herself, the symbolic head of the United Kingdom, who has fairly recent German ancestry (her great-great-grandfather, Queen Victoria's husband, was Albert of Saxe-Coburg and Gotha), and whose husband, Phillip, was himself born in Greece, to a father whose own ancestry was Greek and Russian, and to a mother who, despite being the great-granddaughter of Queen Victoria, lived much of her life in Germany and Greece. Yet who would question Queen Elizabeth II's or Prince Phillip's Englishness? In fact, for some today they represent the very essence of being English. (Though, come to think of it, those who define it otherwise might see what they represent as an impediment to new ways of being English.) So it's just that some of us have been somewhere long enough, repeatedly done the things that people there do, so as to afford us a sense of enduring and exclusive ownership over the place, the practices, the assumptions, etc. I certainly know that by the time I got to grade 12 I had a rather different sense of who I was and how I was related to my high school, than I had when I first walked into that institution upon starting grade 9 – back when I didn't know where anything, or who anyone, was. (In fact, I have a clear memory of being a little lost and asking the Principal, who was patrolling the halls on the first day of school, how to get to my classroom.)

Now, this model of identity formation – one in which familiar context and routine environment create the conditions in which *we come to think of ourselves* as being a this or a that – differs rather dramatically from what I'm calling our day-to-day or commonsense model. For, as already demonstrated at a variety of sites, in this alternative approach we drop references to "expressing yourself" and completely rethink the assumption of identity as being based on an inner, stable center that is only secondarily forced outward into the world. For now it's just the opposite: a world into which we didn't choose to be born creates a framework of limits in which we come to think of ourselves as specific sorts of selves who are related to others in either this or that specific sort of way. And so, instead of that verb "express" we coin new technical terms to signify the ongoing process in which this alternative approach to identify formation understands us all to be involved, each moment of our lives – terms such as "interpellate." Used by some authors in this volume, we associate it with the late Louis Althusser, a mid-twentieth-century French social theorist, who was interested in, among other things, this process of identity formation. But instead of starting with the lone individual, as so many do (think, for a moment, of how we often tend to assume that groups are formed from prior individuals who only later band together – a classic approach associated with much social theory to this day), Althusser – as part of a long line of theorists who emphasize the study of structure over individuals – started with the assumption that the group comes first. While controversial to some, it's hardly a provocative move for theorists who take seriously the powerful role the group has over each of us. For instance, more than likely you didn't choose your name, and you certainly didn't choose your birth order or your birth parents or the socio-economic conditions into which you were born, let alone the country or the time period. Certainly we each exercise choice on a daily basis – "Coffee or tea? Cream and sugar?" – but might the freedom to choose be comparable to the above comments on speed limits? To pick just a quick example, the choice between a hot dog and a hamburger is indeed a choice – picture yourself presented with these options at picnic. But what does the vegetarian say in reply? Or someone who might be fasting or have issues with gluten? For neither is then an option, since such actors play by rather different sets of rules, work within different structures, and are therefore interested in a choice that falls far outside the parameters (i.e., the limits) that have been presented to them at the barbeque.

So Althusser, like other theorists, reversed things, and started with the assumption that identities were made for us by those who surround us – both those who came before us, like older siblings and parents (whose own identities were made for them by yet prior others) and also those who exist today alongside us as peers or as employers or even subordinates at work. So instead of a sense of identity being a projection from the inside out, such scholars theorize that it might instead be the routinized internalization of an outward situation in which we happen to find ourselves – like a brother unexpectedly having his status and thus place challenged when he's home for a visit. And that gets us back to the technical term "interpellation." Derived from a Latin word that conveys the sense of interrupting things (like the often-cited example of interrupting a speech in Parliament in order to ask a question) and, by extension, sometimes used to signify something being slipped in between two other things (such as the discs in our spine being interpellated between the vertebrae), in Althusser's writings we find this term used to name the process whereby institutions and other social actors allow us to be placed into positions that create for us and others what we call an identity. The classic example, of course, is the so-called hail from a police officer mentioned in the introduction – "Hey you there!" – which turns the person who hears it into a suspect (if not criminal) or what we might call "a person of interest." For the authorized speaker – inasmuch as they are seen by us to be in a specific relation to authorized institutions of the state – places the person they're hailing into a specific sort of relationship with themselves and, more importantly, with the institutions they represent/which authorize them (courts, jails, etc.); for there are implications (sometimes severe and possibly deadly) to *not* stopping, to *not* standing still, to *not* taking your hands out of your pockets, to *not* putting your hands up or leaving them in plain sight on the steering wheel, to *not* answering questions posed to you in a respectful tone, etc. While the person him- or herself might not *feel* like a suspect or a criminal (since they think themselves to be, say, a law-abiding member of the middle class just driving home after attending a retirement party) this information is not accessible to the officer; in fact, the person of interest may fit, when seen through the eyes of the officer (who is him or herself interpellated within yet other environments by yet others), the description of someone who might be seen as dangerous. (Should readers – especially US readers – be thinking about the spate of motorists, especially African-Americans, who die at the hands of the police in what might start out as seemingly inconsequential roadside stops, then this provides a powerful example to think through what's happening in the process of identification [an example to which we will certainly return].)

So, for Althusser, identity, or a sense of self, is formed in the give-and-take, negotiated moment when two or more social actors meet (often involving actors who are each placed in different positions along the continuum of authority). As suggested much earlier, in the case of the two squabbling brothers, without that interaction, without the social moment, one could go so far as to suggest that people do not actually have identities in the moment, or perhaps that they merely carry with them, on whatever conscious level, the still-present residue from prior interactions awaiting operationalization if the situation presents itself. Though, if you think about it (and note how, much like the singer discussed earlier, as a writer *I'm making this request of you right now*, making reading no less a social moment in which people and thus social forces interact), when you're not challenged to think about who you are you likely don't much think about who you are. (How tough [maybe impossible?] is it to imagine a moment when you're *not* thinking about who you are, as the experimental test case?) For instance, none of us probably thinks much about how old we are unless we're in a setting where our age is questioned or challenged – such as when you're buying alcohol, perhaps, or trying to get into a club, or maybe trying to do a physical activity that your body no longer can master. Only then do we, as we say, "feel our age." Or, with a nod to the introduction, consider that someone probably doesn't "feel short" until some desired object is just out of reach – i.e., the circumstance creates the identity.

For instance, consider this extended quotation, from Leslie Dorrough Smith:[2]

> Several years ago, at Chipotle, I realized that one of the workers behind the counter was a student of mine, one to whom I'd spoken the week before about his poor performance and a particularly compulsive (and, for me, wildly distracting) propensity to text during class. As we were suspended in an awkward moment where he was asking me what kind of salsa I wanted,

2  This was posted on September 6, 2016 at: https://edge.ua.edu/leslie-dorrough-smith/standing-in-line-at-chipotle-or-the-hefty-politics-of-naming/.

another question came out of his mouth as well: Did he still have to call me "Dr. Smith" when he was at work?

My answer, as I remember it, was stumbling and incoherent, comprised of "uh" and the general surprise of not knowing what to say. On the one hand I didn't really care what he called me, for plenty of my students call me by my first name. On the other hand, though, Dr. Smith was not mentally in the building, so to speak; I was not expecting anyone to call me by my professional title, so I was caught off guard when it came up in a weekend conversation about tacos and corn salsa. But before I could think much more about the significance of what he had asked and how I had responded, the chatter devolved into guacamole and credit cards, and the exchange was over just as fast as it happened.

I've hung on to that memory in great part because it pinpoints how seemingly tentative are the politics of authority at the same time that they endure far beyond our momentary awareness of them. In his well-known volume on the subject, Bruce Lincoln points out that authority is more the *perception* of being in charge rather than actually holding that particular control, for if one is asked to prove one's authority, then it has already begun to erode. In other words, the fact that a different scenario has entered the minds of those doing the asking indicates that they have begun to scrutinize the power status quo.

This was, after all, what was going on in that brief exchange. While I thought it somewhat impertinent to point out that his job didn't require knowing his customers' names, my name was not at issue as much as the disappearance of the political context that marked our previous relationship, one where I was not only "in charge," but had also asserted some of that authority in a way that had recently highlighted his shortcomings. His questioning of my name thus introduced the possibility that our politics might be reversed or at least neutralized in a setting that was more "his turf" than mine, and I suppose in so doing, to potentially de-legitimize the critiques he'd recently experienced.

And yet what stands out to me in all of this is the enduring power of interpellation, that term Althusser used to discuss the ways in which we almost subconsciously submit to the classificatory schema that society imposes upon us. In his famous example of a policeman yelling "Hey, you!," Althusser demonstrates that the moment we give ourselves over to the possibility that we are the "you" in question and start to turn around to face (and thereby accept) the label, we demonstrate how imminently social our identities are – how very much they are the products of forces far outside of our own creation. In this case, even though I failed to give a coherent answer to the student's question in that moment, I did not fail to be a professor. In other words, I could not ignore the fact that "Dr. Smith" was with "Leslie" at Chipotle that day.

What Smith so nicely illustrates, in this seemingly mundane moment at a fast-food restaurant, is that identity can be studied as the effect of the situations in which people do not *project an identity* but, rather, *are identified* by others, by means of this process of interpellation – that is, are brought into the types of relationships that prompt them to feel young or old, to feel male or female (or, yes, transgender), to experience themselves as having a race, a nationality – even to see themselves as a customer as opposed to a professor! Instead of starting with the assumption that identity is an ethereal, non-empirical, and perhaps just naturally occurring inner experience, we now begin anew, by looking at the social settings where people interact, looking for cues and occasions by which they make each other into a this or a that. As another example, remember the introduction's reference to an unexpected knock on your door at home – until that knock you were more than likely not experiencing yourself as a host, but in the moment of that rapping on your door, or ringing of your doorbell, you suddenly become concerned for how neat your apartment is or how well you are (or are not) dressed. For until that precise moment you were not put into the position (and it is indeed a position you were *put into*) of needing to entertain someone (and thereby allow them to see the cluttered living room of someone midway through a weekend Netflix binge). But now, simply in the light of a knock on your door, you must suddenly adopt the role of host, ready to entertain, even if that only means opening the door to speak to someone. ("Do I have anything to offer them?

Soda? Maybe some chips...?") For, prior to that moment, you were just unthinkingly wearing whatever it was that you were happening to wear, and your place looked however it happens to look on a Saturday morning or a Tuesday night. But, with that rap rap rap on the door, you unexpectedly prepare to be judged by whomever it is who will peer through the open door to see what has, in your mind at least, suddenly become a messy place – the messiness, of course, is not a natural quality but a brand new social judgment that we ourselves make by imagining how an unannounced visitor might see it.

I could offer other examples, of course, but my hope is that readers can provide plenty of their own; instances where identity (such as the living room's "messiness," to stick with what might be an easily digested example – after all, not just people have identities, correct?) can be entertained as an attribute *given to things or to people by means of the relationships and situations into which they've been put*. Change the relationship, alter the situation, tweak the structure, and the identity – the sense of our place which we have gained from the cues and prompts that surround us – will change. Sooner or later – thinking back to that earlier example from the British exit from the EU – we will come to feel like we belong, as if we are legitimate and at home, or, conversely, as out of place, foreign, estranged, or illegitimate ("When we were kids you would've called it *macaroni*!"). Identity, then, becomes a continually collaborative project, in which we and all others constantly participate, signaling (often unknowingly) to those who are our peers, our inferiors, and our supervisors, information about how we are intertwined with each other – that we overlap or are diverse, that we share things in common or are alien to one another. And, whatever the outcome at this moment, when situations change, so too will the identities that derive from them – e.g., when two cross-town rivals happen to meet in some foreign country, where they each don't speak the language (that is, where they are each equally alienated from their usually taken-for-granted world) they find themselves quickly becoming fast friends, at least so long as they remain in alien territory. In a word, they now identify *with* each other because they have been identified *by* each other.

And it's this ability to pick and choose (within pre-set limits and based on criteria that happen to be relevant, and thus operative, at any given moment, dictated by each changeable situation), from among the innumerable traits and factors that do or do not overlap at any given site, that allows us to form judgments of similarity (even sameness) or difference; as just suggested, when at home the two US college sports fans perceive themselves to be so different as to be opposed to one another, but spotting each other while both are standing at a ticket counter in Paris, trying to get on a train but not speaking any French, they easily overlook what once counted as a difference and now welcome each other as fellow countrymen able to commiserate because they can speak English to one another. Foe magically becomes friend – but it's not really magic at all. For differing settings, and the new position in which we find ourselves, allow us to operationalize different criteria in our social interactions, all in order to manage that continually shifting set of similarities and differences that simultaneously unite/estrange us to/from all others – thereby creating different selves and different identities; and thanks to this shift in our approach, this always ongoing process now becomes the fascinating thing that we can now begin to study, so long as we see identity not as an invisible quality lurking only on the inside but as the result of all too observable, public situations and changeable factors. And thus we come to see that the opening quotation from Polonius (who is often seen by readers of the play as a fool) might be far more correct than we at first thought – but only if we tweak it just a bit; for not just clothes but also innumerable other items and people in our context *make* – and don't just *proclaim* – us who we are taken to be.

So, if we make this shift then among the things that we now can inquire about are the reasons why we often each perceive ourselves to have identities that endure – that is, why would we read Polonius as shallow in making his observation, and why would we assume that clothes are mere window-trimming on our essential selves? (After all, "Dress for success" is an old saying, no?) For the commonsense model that we usually employ doesn't come from nowhere – in fact, the widespread nature of this very model is something we're now able to study. For if we are each constantly moving from one situation to another, from one set of relationships to various others, *why do we each perceive ourselves as having a constant and uniform identity?* Thinking back to the Latin roots of the term "identity," why do we see ourselves and others to continually be the same? Why are we so surprised to see someone with a new haircut or why, as a kid, did I run around the house, after returning from a few weeks away at summer camp, trying to find the things that had changed? If I think about it, I likely know that the world that I inhabit now is so very different from the one that surrounded me as a small boy that the fact that I so easily conclude that the boy in the framed photo, over on the bookshelf of my cluttered office, "is me" is rather curious indeed. So something that our alternative approach to conceptualizing identity (that is, seeing it as the result of constant and continually changing interpellation) must explain is *why so many of us even arrive at, and work with, the commonsense model in the first place.* Could it be so simple as to say that we are each engaged in a project to authorize one of the many shifting identities that we each have placed upon us, as we move through a continually shifting landscape? For even routinized settings, in which we and others "get used to" behaving and relating to each other in certain ways, don't account for why we and others seem so easily to overlook the contradictions, paying little attention to aspects of ourselves and others that defy the way we usually see each other. (Come to think of it, why was that younger brother so interested to establish his older sibling's difference from the group at home?) But should there be some demonstrable advantage to emphasizing one aspect over all others, then perhaps we can begin to understand why, in a world of continually shifting contexts, and thus regularly revised identities, the vast majority of us work so hard to, for instance, look the same each morning as we stand in front of the mirror or to retroject backward in time our current understanding of ourselves and our place in the world, as if we were always this thing we now happen to be.

Now, some of us don't invest this labor, of course – in fact, given how much of social life is focused on sameness across time some could be said to work just as hard to undermine or call into question the impression that they are each uniform or homogeneous things, thereby troubling assumptions that we each have a specific, singular, and enduring identity. (Do you know people who dye their hair dramatically different colors on a regular basis or frequently change jobs and move cities?) While the prominence in the media, in just the past year or so, of transgender identities – at least here in the US news – could be one place where we could explore this alternative approach to identification, for the time being consider a different example. For at the time of writing this the US's 2016 Republican and Democratic conventions have just taken place, as part of the process to select these parties' candidates to run for President in the Fall. At the latter convention, where a far left, social democratic candidate (Bernie Sanders) lost to a more centrist candidate (Hillary Clinton), a narrative arose in the media of young, nihilistic Sanders supporters who were intent on opting out of (and thereby undermining the chances of) the Democratic Party. To explore whether this narrative was accurate, a group of young delegates were interviewed online by *The Atlantic*, a current events and news magazine; among them was Kendrick Sampson, an actor from California. He replied:

> We have an either/or type of society…. And it's very binary and that's not how humans work. I am angry and I'm fed-up, and I'm sad and I'm hurt. And I'm hopeful and I'm happy. You know, and I can have all those….

At which point the interviewer (Alex Wagner, senior editor for *The Atlantic*), sympathetic to this multivalent approach to identification, interjected, ironically: "That's so many different things at the same time." Sampson responded to her: "I'm a human, you know what I mean? That's how it works."[3]

I find this exchange to be yet another useful example to consider. For, like the way in which transgender identities are now understood to critique the limited, either/or nature of the way we usually

3 The brief video, which interviews several young delegates, is entitled "Bernie or Bargain," posted on July 28, 2016, at http://www.theatlantic. com/video/index/493370/bernie-or-bargain/ (accessed July 29, 2016).

classify and thereby sort ourselves into male and female (a binary system, inasmuch as one must be one or the other, making each mutually exclusive options, like hot and cold or on and off), so too Sampson makes evident that his own identity, as a young Democrat, is far more complex, multivalent, and thus shifting than the conventional media narrative portrays it. With current political events in mind, such as when the Black Lives Matter movement is often portrayed in the popular press as being opposed to what soon after emerged as the pro-law-enforcement Blue Lives Matter movement, a variety of people have come out to argue that one can be a strong supporter of the police *while also* wanting people not to be killed by police officers at traffic stops for broken tail lights. One can support both things, is the message – a message Sampson seems to echo in his description of himself as constituted by simultaneously-existing emotions that might strike many as irreconcilable opposites of one another (i.e., one can be either happy or sad *but not both*). But what makes this all the more interesting is that such efforts to transcend what are portrayed by some as the limitations of binary thinking seem to land us back in but a new binary system: for instance, you either are or are not able to understand the traditional gender identities of male and female as confining and restricting. Though it may sound flippant, we arrive at a moment when it seems that, on the one hand, there are *those who think in terms of binaries* and, on the other, *those who do not* – which is itself but a new binary, operating at a higher level, perhaps, but a set of mutually exclusive positions nonetheless. Case in point: there are those in the US who champion transgender people using the bathroom of the gender with which they currently identify, while there are those who oppose this and insist that the gender recorded on their birth certificate ought to dictate which public washroom they are legally allowed to use (in fact the state of North Carolina currently has enshrined the latter in law).

A classic critique of binary logic, that still has influence, was that of the late literary critic Edward Said, who examined how the Muslim world (once called "the Orient" by Europeans) was generally portrayed (or, as he might have said, caricatured) in European literature from a century or two ago – or even to this day, some would argue. He repurposed the well-known term Orient (deriving from Latin, for east) such that we today discuss how Orientalism is a strategy to define self by creating a self-serving representation of the Other, against whom one then defines oneself as different. For if, despite internal differences among those considered alien to us, we can portray some uniform "them" as, let's just say, irrational, then "we" are rational, and so on, and so on. This us/them binary logic, and the role played by representation in our own creation of a self-beneficial image of an Other, seems to name a basic human identification technique; to put it in other words, if a theorist like Althusser is correct, and identity is in fact a constantly negotiated social practice involving two or more agents, and, furthermore, if you and I are continually moving from relationship to relationship and from setting to setting, thus implicating us in innumerable different identities in the course of just one day, then a strategy might be needed if we are incapable of entertaining that vague ambivalence and utter heterogeneity may be the best way to characterize daily life. If so, then the process examined by Said, what he just termed Orientalism, may make evident the way that each of us grapples with ambiguity and change, a grappling that creates for us the far more manageable impression of possessing a uniform, stable self that is easily distinguishable from the equally uniform and stable selves supposedly possessed by everyone else. If this is persuasive, then the commonsense model that each of us adopts, whereby we just seem to intuitively know that the youthful photo is a picture of us, may itself be a technique that we, as human beings, employ to make sense of, or rather to manage, a world that might be far more fluid and even contradictory than we generally realize. Orientalism, when expanded far beyond how Europeans once characterized Muslims to their own benefit, might therefore name a fundamental way in which we all signify (i.e., make meaningful) the world in order to live in it, so that we can start here now and get to there then – using clocks and compasses, maps and itineraries to order and thereby characterize a centerless and thus borderless reality *as if* it has clear limits and precise edges. For, if you think about it, we know that we will never reach the horizon, inasmuch as it continually retreats as we advance our way around the globe – unless, that is, we arbitrarily establish a fixed point in the distance, a destination, toward which we can aim. And now, so long as we grant the legitimacy of that point, we'll know when we're closer to or further from it, and when we've arrived at it. But this fixed point, of course, merely reflects the interests of whomever it was who planted that flag into the ground – and those happenstance interests can be lost, forgotten, overlooked, such that we eventually might either ignore it altogether, while planting a few flags of our own, or, instead, we might take the flag's presence as self-evident, maybe even necessary or inevitable, thereby failing to see it as a device someone once used to create their own impression of a center, a target, a point to focus upon, and thus a way to organize some region that they created.

If so, then Orientalism (defined as self-serving representations that create the impression of an Other different from Self) might be inevitable to us (and useful for all sorts of differing purposes, to be sure); for it might name the process whereby we create the *impression* of stable points of difference – whether on a map or between people – meaning that it is another way to say what others might just term identification, even signification.

But at this point I should stop, and retreat to my opening example, of two brothers contesting and defending place. I've suggested that, contrary to how we normally see it, the process of identification is social, is collaborative, implies multiple actors of different levels of authority, all interacting in constantly shifting contexts and thus deriving constantly shifting senses of how they either are or are not related to all others who surround them. And as a response to this blur of activity, I've argued that actors seem to simplify the many worlds they inhabit, just in order to get on with the business of living a life, thereby presenting to themselves and others the impression of uniformity and constancy. And this, I've concluded, is perhaps just how meaning-making (that is, signification) works, ensuring that we now see identity as but a subspecies of how it is that we, as human beings, make meaning. For of all the sounds we make we will limit just some to be language, and of all the symbols that we can create we will limit just some to be letters – and working within that system of limitation we will creatively and almost endlessly combine them all, the vowels and the consonants, to make the rich meanings that come out of our mouths or are otherwise performed by our bodies (such as the typing I'm doing right now, not to mention the reading you're doing). This is a process that requires us to overlook ambiguity and difference, calls on us to accept, and thus not even see, the structure within which we live – for now we can get on with the business of just reading the owner's manual to find out how to turn the car's wipers on and off. What I'm therefore suggesting is that we can think critically about how it is that we each come to perceive ourselves as having an identity if we also consider thinking critically about how it is that readers think what they're now seeing on this page is meaningful. For in both cases there may be something more going on than the commonsense model tells us – for the meaning might not be *in the words* so much as *in the circulation of grammar rules in the interacting minds of readers*, just as the thing we perceive as identity *may not be in us* so much as *in the circulation and interaction of multiple bodies in controlled but changing situations*.

I'm not sure whether this is as much a conclusion as it is a repetition of the underlying points that the authors in this book have each been exploring – explorations that are themselves spots where they are investigating an alternative approach, indebted not just to Althusser but also to such scholars as Judith Butler (who famously argued that gendered identity is the result of how we each perform ourselves for each other) and, more recently, Jean François Bayart (whose work was mentioned in the introduction and, like Butler, discussed throughout the chapters). But, come to think of it, the presumption that there's been an "underlying point" across the otherwise diverse authors and chapters in this book may be but one more data point that needs exploration if what I've argued up to now is persuasive; after all, this very afterword is intent on making meaning no less than any other cultural act, and has worked to bring together a diverse collection of writers who have all explored different sites. That suggests that our theory of identification should apply here no less than anywhere else – no less than a 1970s funk song in the midst of social upheaval or two brothers trying to determine what continues to unite them as adults. But I leave that application to you, the reader – if, that is, you agree that our commonsense model for thinking and talking about who we are is more curious than we usually realize.


Russell T. McCutcheon is Professor and Chair of the Department of Religious Studies at the University of Alabama. He has published widely on the study of religion's history and the politics of classification – specifically the socio-political uses of the taxon "religion" (whether employed as a folk or technical term).

# Index

*30 Rock*, 107
9/11, 36

academic
  as collaborative, 116 ff., 119 ff.
  as contested, 116 ff.
  as identity, 116 ff., 121
adult/child, 3 ff., 24 ff., 32, 36, 76,
  102, 105 ff., 112–13
adulting, 112
agency
  as liberal form, 57
  theory of, 58
agnostic, perennial, 133
AIPAC (American Israel Public
  Affairs Committee), 27
Alabama, 83 ff.
  caricature of, 82, 89 ff.
  civil rights, 85
  history, 83, 89–90
  as identity, 82, 89 ff.
  perceptions of, 89
alchemy, 13
Althusser, Louis, 3, 17, 99,
  120, 151–5, 163; see also:
  Ideological State Apparatus,
  interpellation
American Academy of Religion
  (AAR), 59
American religions, as identifiable
  area of study, 124

Anglican Church of Ireland, 35
Annie E. Casey Foundation, 85
anthropology, 77, 112
apostasy, as crime, 67
area studies, 11, 13
Armenian massacre, 7
assimilation, 27
astronomy, 13
atheism, 47, 66 ff.
  discrimination of, 71
  as divisive, 69
  as identity, 66 ff., 133
  as militant, 69–70
  as nasty thing, 69
  New Atheism, 69–70
  in politics, 68–9
  in the US, 68
Atheist Shoes, 70–1
*Atlantic, The*, 159
Aurelius, Marcus, 117
authenticity, 6, 10, 12, 34, 56, 117,
  132, 141
  as authentic self, 38, 143
  as inauthentic, 147
  in parenting, 108–9
  as real, 37
authority, 21, 152
  claims of, 101
  as constructed, 102
  as continuum, 153
  politics of, 154

autonomy, 56, 79; see also: choice
Aykroyd, Dan, 109

baby, 105 ff.
　as universal, 109
baptism
　as naming, 96
"Bathroom Bill" (Public Facilities
　Privacy & Security Act [North
　Carolina]), 160
Bayart, Jean-François, 1, 5, 7–8,
　40, 56, 100, 111, 123, 133, 163
beauty/appearance
　as constructed, 128
　as identity, 128–9
　as patriarchal, 129
　power dynamics of, 128 ff.
belief
　as communal, 78
　disbelief, 70
　in God or higher powers, 70, 72
　as individual, 66
　lack of, 66 ff.
Belluck, Pam, 55
Bible, the, 24, 61
Bible belt, 24, 84
binary, 159–61
　as mutually exclusive, 160
Black Lives Matter movement, 92,
　103, 160
blackness, as criminalized, 102
blasphemy laws, 67–68
Blue Lives Matter movement, 160
border, 161
　US/Canada, 83
Borges, Jorge Luis, 120, 122–3
boundaries
　as constructed, 94
　us/them (see also: us/them), 89,
　161

Bourdieu, Pierre, 56, 116, 121
Boy Scouts, 43
Braun, Willi, 31
Brexit, 39, 148–9, 156
Brown, Wendy, 116, 121
Browning, Robert, 122
Buddhism, 66
Burton, LeVar, 102–3
Butler, Judith, 58, 113, 116, 121,
　163

Calvino, Italo, 121
Canada, 86, 95, 111, 140
　as "Great White North," 86
　as identity, 83, 132–3, 140, 149
　as myth, 137
Canadian Charter of Rights and
　Freedoms [1982], 69
capitalism, 87, 111
　as built on slavery, 87
　as global, 145
categories, as local, 97
center/margin, 5, 112
　as majority, 135
Charles Wright & the Watts 103rd
　Street Rhythm Band, 143
childhood
　as constructed, 112
　as flexible category, 114
　as identity, 112–14
　as play, 112
choice, 157
　as freedom, 79, 151
　as individual, 79, 151
　as limited, 157
Chomsky, Noam, 18
Christianity, 15, 35ff., 63, 66, 77,
　79
　as American, 78, 91
　as Catholic, 35–6, 78

as cultural practice, 91
as Greek Orthodox, 96, 99
as Protestant, 35–6, 70
as Puritan, 45
church and state, separation of, 48
citation
  as agenda, 121
  as construction of past in present, 122
  as context-dependent, 123
  as identity, 122–3
civil rights, 84, 147
  history of, 85
  "a Southern problem," 85
civility/barbarity, 17
claims, 8
  as act of identification, 125
  of authority (see also: authority), 101
  of truth, 66
class, 22, 108, 112, 134, 140
classification, 3, 46, 77, 113–14, 124, 155
  as attempt to delegitimize, 117
  as context-dependent, 45
  as naming, 97, 101
  as United Kingdom or Great Britain, 39
Clifford, James, 8
Clinton, Hillary, 159
CNN (Cable News Network), 103
colonialism, 16, 26
commodification, 15
community
  communal consciousness, 7–8
  idea of, 7
comparison, 43, 45, 46, 109
  as context dependent, 43
  as interpretation, 46
  as strategic, 117

Concerned Women for America (CWA), 63
conflict, as racialized, 103
conscious ignoring, 90 ff.
  examples of, 90
  as "public secret," 91
conspiracy theories, 14, 16, 17
Constantinople, 7
content, as function of context, 145
contingency, 8
  of identity, 126, 138, 144, 150, 153, 159
contradiction, 145–6
cosmopolitanism, 27
cotton industry, 86 ff.
Cox, James, 14, 15
credibility, 123
creolization, 5
crystals, 19
culture
  as constructed, 78, 100, 135
  defined, 5
  as essentialized, 108
  as food, 73
  as heteronormative, 129
  perspective, 46
  sociological critique of, 23, 100
Culture on the Edge, 1–2, 4, 6, 110, 118, 124–5

data
  identification practices as, 139 ff.
  as not intrinsically interesting, 57
Dawkins, Richard, 69, 133
de Certeau, Michel, 38
demystification, 49
Dennett, Daniel, 69
Derrida, Jacques, 116, 121
designation, 1
diaspora, 5, 97

difference (see also: similarity), 24,
  27, 83, 124–5, 130, 157
  as imagined, 162
  in parenting, 107
  as regional, 84
  as rhetoric, 124
distinction, 57
  as local, 83–4
  as territory, 36
dreamcatchers, 19
Durkheim, Emile, 1, 116–17, 121

education system, 83
emotion, 2
England
  as essentialized, 149
  as identity, 149
  as non-English, 149
essentialism, viii, 16, 37, 149
  of culture, 108
  of identity (see: identity)
  as illusion, 8
  of naming, 95, 98
  of self, 157
ethnicity, 7, 103, 124
European Union (EU), 39–40,
  148–9, 156
experience, 93, 117
  in academia, 125
  as collaborative, 146
  as lived, 66
  of motherhood, 108
  as religious, 2
explanation, 8
expression, 2, 139 ff.
  express yourself, 6, 139 ff.
  of identity (see also: identity, as
    secondary expression), 2, 33,
    120, 124, 139 ff.
  as public, 145

faith, 117
"fake it till you make it," 56 ff.
feminism, 61 ff.
  as divisive, 62
  feminist movement, 147
  as identity (feminist), 61
  as nasty thing, 62
  as resistance or emancipation, 57
feminist studies, 61
Fitzgerald, Timothy, 17, 19
flags (national) as identity, 36 ff.,
  162
Floyd, Pink, 117
folklore, 31
food
  as class based, 140
  as identity, 73 ff., 77 ff., 140
  as practice, 78–9, 80
  as religion, 77–9
  as tradition, 80, 81
food studies, 77
*Forrest Gump*, 85
Foucault, Michel, 116, 121
freedom
  created by intersection of rules
    and systems, 147
  as fabricated, 146
  as ideal, 93
  as inherent to the US, 93
  as ironic reward, 101
  as limited, 146, 151
  as rights (US), 92, 146
Freud, Sigmund, 116–17
future, as imagined, 4

Gandhi, Mohandas, 117
Gen X, 20 ff.
gender, 10, 51 ff., 61, 108, 139
  as binary, 160
  as cis-gender, 113

as classification, 113–14
discourses on, 108
gender equity, 61–2
as fluid, 113
as identity, 113
as performative, 113
as power, 134, 136
rhetoric, 131
versus sex, 113
as transgender, 159
generalizations, 21
ghost in the machine, 2
ghosts, belief in, 15
Gnosticism, 14
Golden Age of Pericles, 29–30
Google Scholar, 121–2
Great Depression, 80
Greece, 28
 ancient Greece, 30
 Athena (Αθηνα), 96
 Athens (Αθήνα), 29, 96
 as diaspora, 96
 Greek identity, 29 ff., 96,
  99–100
 language, 96–7, 99
 modern Greece, 30
 naming, 95 ff., 99
 National Celebration, 32
 Souli (Greek folklore), 31
 Thessaloniki, 29
Grimes, Ronald L., 101
Groubert, Sean, 102
gun laws, 83

Harper, Stephen, 137
Harris, Sam, 69
healthcare system, 83
Hebrew Bible, 24
 characters in, 25
heretic, 133

heritage
 festival, 96
 French Canadian, 138
 Greek, 29–30
 Irish, 132
heteronormativity
 as power, 129, 134, 136
Hinduism, 47, 77, 79
hip hop, 20
history
 African American, 101
 as alternative, 93
 as ancient, 30
 as cautionary tale, 101
 as collaborative, 88
 as national, 35
 of Northern Ireland, 35 ff.
 as popular memory, 31
 as social formation, 31
 of US, 90 ff.
Hitchens, Christopher, 69
Holocaust, the, 25–6
Holocaust Remembrance Day
 (Yom HaShoah), 24
homeopathy, 19
Hubbard, L. Ron, 16
Hughes, Aaron, 11–12, 37
humanities, 11, 27, 119
hybridity, 5
hypocrisy, 63

Icke, David, 16
ID card, 95, 99 ff.
identification
 operational acts, 1, 23, 36, 40,
  41, 44, 58, 63, 76, 78, 89, 93,
  100, 103, 111, 114, 116–18,
  119 ff., 128 ff., 133, 139 ff.
 resistance to, 23, 70–2, 101, 118,
  128

self-identification, 8, 29 ff., 35
　ff. 42, 63–4, 67–8, 70–2, 73
　ff., 76, 81, 82, 89 ff., 93, 95
　ff., 101, 102, 116 ff., 119 ff.,
　128, 132 ff.
　strategies, 6, 38, 66, 71, 76, 83,
　　96, 111, 128 ff., 139 ff.
　as tactical, 38, 139 ff.
identification as object of study,
　139, 150–1
　as different from commonsense
　　approach, 157
　requiring self-consciousness, 139
identity
　as academic influence, 116–17,
　　119 ff.
　as appearance/beauty, 128 ff.
　as behavior, 51 ff.
　as career, 83
　as claimed, 140
　as collaboration, 3, 38, 42, 50,
　　76, 78, 80, 83, 95 ff., 102,
　　113–14, 116, 119 ff., 132 ff.,
　　139 ff.
　as collective, 92, 135
　as consequential, 68, 71, 86
　as contingent, 126, 138, 144,
　　150, 158
　economically based, 80, 151
　as empirically observable thing,
　　51
　as fabricated, 58, 75, 100, 113,
　　119–20, 122–3, 126, 132, 135,
　　139, 151
　as feminist, 61 ff.
　as fixed, stable, or static, 38, 108,
　　112, 119, 125, 139, 144, 158
　as fluid, 31, 43, 53, 56, 76, 93,
　　133, 141–1, 147–8, 153–5,
　　158, 162

folk model, 2
　as food, 73 ff., 77 ff., 140
　as gendered, 53–4, 107, 113–14,
　　134, 163
　as historical, 23, 31, 92, 126, 144
　identity-making, 56, 102, 139,
　　151
　as individual or unique, 144
　as indoctrination, 55
　as internalized, 151
　as intrinsic, 33, 43, 79, 139 ff.
　as learned, 102
　as localized, 83, 93
　many identities, 28, 119, 132 ff.
　as marginalized, 80–1
　as mental fact, 8
　as national, 28, 36, 82–3, 92,
　　133, 135–7, 149–50
　as natural, 53, 105 ff., 139
　having normative associations,
　　117
　as not random, 27
　as official, 95, 98, 100
　as other, 36, 85 ff., 89
　as pejorative, 117, 124
　as performance, 23, 31, 51 ff.,
　　55, 58, 106, 113–14, 144, 163
　as policed, 100 ff.
　as pretend, 55–6
　as primordial, 8, 56
　as privilege, 134–5, 138
　as racial, 86, 100 ff.
　as response, 147, 153
　as secondary expression, 2, 33,
　　120, 124, 139 ff.
　as seeming natural, 53, 105 ff.,
　　139
　as sexually oriented, 54, 55
　as situated, 126, 133, 142, 147,
　　150, 153

as taken-for-granted, 141
as taxonomic category, 152, 139 ff.
universality, notion of, 106
as urban, 100
as vague, 74
as verb, 6
as weird thing, 20
identity politics, 35 ff., 62–4, 74, 78, 100 ff., 111, 117, 119 ff., 139 ff.
Ideological State Apparatus (ISA), 17; see also: Althusser, Louis, interpellation
immigration, 86, 149–50
imposter syndrome, 58, 147
Indigenous cultures, 80, 137
   rights of, 86
individual, 79–80, 151
   belief, 66
   as capitalistic, 111
   choice, 79–80
   versus group, 93
   as identity, 144
   as liberal, 137
Industrial Revolution, 86–7
inherited characteristic, 43, 46
*Inside Out*, 2
insider/outsider problem, 84, 106, 110–11, 138, 140, 149
interdisciplinarity, 10, 12
interfaith dialogue, 15, 17
interpellation, 3 ff., 99 ff., 120, 151–5, 158; see also: Althusser, Louis, Ideological State Apparatus
interpretation
   act of, 46, 79
   necessary for translation, 46
   as strategic, 46

Iordanidu, Maria, 7
Irby, James, 119
Ireland, 67, 132
   Irish identity, 38, 132
   Northern, 34 ff.
   Republic of, 35, 37, 38, 39
Islam/Muslim(s), 15, 19, 36, 47, 58, 77, 90, 161
   controversy surrounding hijab, 137
   as identity, 47, 77, 118, 137, 139
   and Orientalism, 160–1
Israel, 25–6
   as Promised Land, 25

Jainism, 77
Jesus, 46, 61, 117
Jones, Levar, 102–3
Judaism, 24 ff., 77
   African Jews, 26
   American Jewry, 25, 27
   as distinctive area of study, 124
   Jewish identity, 23 ff.
   Jewish law, 26
   as political, 26
   Reform, 24

Kafka, Franz, 122
Kant, Immanuel, 117
Kennedy, Bobby (Robert F.), 147
Kennedy, John F., 85
Kenny, Mary Lorena, 112
Kierkegaard, Soren, 122
King, Martin Luther, Jr., 147
Krukkert, Sanne, 149
Kunta Kinte, 101–2

labels, 42 ff., 45 ff., 64, 66, 69–71, 73, 75, 117–18, 129, 131, 134, 135, 138

as complex, 71, 73–5
as consequential, 67, 71
as constructed, 49
as contested, 46, 71, 118
having ethical or moral component, 73, 76
as fluid, 71
power of, 71
process of labeling, 45–7, 49–50, 76
self-selected, 42, 75
as tricky, 49
Lacan, Jacques, 116–17
Lakota, 80
Lancy, David F., 112
language
etymology of "express," 142
etymology of "interpellation," 151
as identity, 142
as meaning-making, 163
law
dictated by state, 101, 146
interpretation of, 101
as libel, 146
Lemon, Liz, 107
Leno, Jay, caricature of, 89
Liechty, Joseph and Celia Clegg, 35
Lincoln, Bruce, 154
Locke, John, 68
Lombard, Denys, 7
Louis C.K., 135
*Loving v. Virginia* (1967), 102

Macedonians, 30
MacKinnon, Catherine, 129
Mahmood, Saba, 57–8
manliness, 52

marriage
as interracial, 102
licenses of, 102
as privilege, 102
as same-sex, 102
Martin, Craig, 23, 37, 62, 119 ff.
Marx, Karl, 116–17, 121
masculinity, 11
Maurios, André, 122
McCutcheon, Russell T., 17, 55, 56, 89 ff., 99, 110, 116 ff., 119 ff.
McCutcheonite
as academic influence, 116, 119 ff.
as classification, 117
as identity, 116 ff., 119 ff.
as pejorative, 117, 124
McGarry, John and Brendan O'Leary, 35
McLuhan, Marshall, 145
meaning, 6, 36, 163
meaning-making, 47, 161–2
methodological agnosticism, 17
millennials, 21–2
entitlement, 21
Miller, Monica, 98
Molson Brewing Company, 135–7
morality, 58
motherhood, 105 ff.
as contested, 106
discourse on, 106
as identity, 105, 108, 111–12
as shared experience, 108
MTV (Music Television), 21
Mullholland, Marc, 35

name, 95 ff.
as Christian, 101
as code-switching, 98

as contested, 99
forename, 95 ff.
as identity, 95 ff., 154–5
naming processes, 47, 62–4, 99
as notion of "essential core,"
    95, 98
as policing mechanism, 97
pronunciation, 95
surname, 97
as title, 148, 154–5
narrative, 4, 93
as competing, 46
as constructed, 29ff., 35
as fabricated, 36
generation, 21–2
in Hebrew Bible, 25
of Judaism, 26
of origins, 46
as self-serving, 27
as story-telling, 45
as strategy, 46
National Public Radio (NPR), 148
nationalism
ethno-nationalism, 26
as performance, 30 ff.
Nazi ideology, 27
"Negro question, the," 103
neo-pagan, 47
as distinctive area of study, 124
New Age, 14, 15
New Testament, 14
normativity, 17, 117
as heteronormative, 129, 134,
    136
Nosaprise (Nosa Edebor), 100

Obama, Barack, 20
caricature of, 89
*Obergefell v. Hodges* (2015), 102
oppression as identity-based, 61

Orange, William of, 35
Orientalism
as caricature, 160
as east, 161
as other, 161–2
origin, 5, 43
as narrative, 46
requiring notion of continuity,
    43
Ott, Julia, 87
Ottoman Empire, 30 ff.

parent(ing), 105, 114
as "Attachment Parent," 106
as "Authoritative Parent," 106
differences, 107
division of labor, 107
as identity, 105 ff., 110
progressive style, 108
pasta
as a class-based food, 140
as macaroni, 140, 156
Patrick, Jeremy, 67
pedagogy, 51 ff., 66–7
as ethical, 58
perception
as culturally determined, 46
performativity, 58–9, 140, 163
of gender, 113
of identity, 23, 31, 51 ff., 55, 58,
    106, 113–14, 144, 163
of nationalism, 30
of religion, 27
of ritual, 140
of social groups, 140–1
periphery, 39
perspective, 43–4
as counter-story, 46
as selected perception, 45
Petrou, Ioannis, 95

Pew Research Center, 21, 68
piety, 58
police (law enforcement)
  as identity, 152
  killings, 101, 152
  as power, 100–1
Polonius (*Hamlet*), 139, 157
power, 26, 38, 63, 87
  as ambiguous, 134
  dynamics of, 100 ff., 128 ff.
  ethics as means of, 58
  as gendered, 129,134, 136
  as hegemonic, 38, 39
  as heteronormative, 129 ff., 134,
    136
  as malleable, 134
  as order, 101
  as patriarchal, 57, 128 ff.
  as police, 100–1
  as psychological, 26
  as racial, 100 ff.
  as rhetorical, 62, 131
  as self-determination, 80
practices, 66, 78
  as communal, 78
  as ethical, 80
  as fluid, 78
  of food, 78–9, 80
  as religious, 78, 80
  as secular, 78
pregnancy, 105–6
primordiality, 6, 7–8
privilege, 138
  as cis-gender, 134–5
  as male, 54, 134–5
  of marriage, 102
  as white, 134–5
profane (see also: sacred), 58
psychoanalysis, 116

Queen Elizabeth, UK, 150
  ancestry of, 150

race, 10, 22, 86–87, 100–2
  melanin content of skin as indi-
    cator, 20, 23
  relations, 147
"race card," 100
racism, 100
  national history (US), 92
  rhetoric, 137
  "as Southern thing," 90
Ramey, Steven, 45, 46, 49–50,
  76–7, 79
reality effect, 56
reductionism, 118
reincarnation, 15
religion
  alternative, 14
  as choice, 79
  as constructed, 49
  as contested, 27, 48–9, 78, 79
  definition of, 13, 49
  discourses, 37, 110
  as false, 48–9
  food practices of, 77–9
  historicized, 14
  ideological category, 17
  indigenous, 15, 18
  material, 15
  new, 14, 18; new religious
    movements, 18
  non-religion/religious, 47–8,
    70 ff., 133
  as performance, 27
  as practice, 26, 78
  real religion, 13
  as system of values, 48–9
  as taxonomic category, 11, 84,
    117, 125

world religions paradigm, 15,
17, 19, 47, 77
religious studies
as discipline, 10 ff., 46 ff., 67,
77, 79, 84, 110–11
discourse on religion as data,
110–11
lacking distinctive method, 13
resistance
as social, 62–4
rhetoric, 15, 31
of difference, 124
of gender, 131
of power, 62, 131
of race, 137
as strategic, 62
ritual, 77
as performance, 140
rock and roll, 20
*Roots* (1977), 101–2
Ruane, Joseph and Jennifer Todd,
35

sacred (see also: profane), 58,
108–9
Said, Edward, 160–1
Sampson, Kendrick, 159–60
Sanders, Bernie, 159
Santería, 78
Schaeffer, Frank, 70
Scheper-Hughes, Nancy, 112
*Schindler's List*, 24
Scottish Independence, 38
Scrooge, Ebenezer, 42, 45, 46
secularization, 14
Segal, Robert, 13, 18
segregation, enforced, 92
self (see also: identity)
as authentic, 143

as constructed, 121, 153
critical awareness, 47
essential, 157
as interpreted, 121
policing, 100 ff.
reflection, 139, 141
as situated, 141, 153
as social 2, 4, 147, 153
as stable, 6
sexism, 61, 128 ff.
"Sexy School Girl" Halloween
costume, 129
Shakespeare, William, 130
"short and cute"
as classification, 134
as difference, 131
as gendered, 129
as identity, 128
power dynamics of, 128 ff.
subliminal symbolism of, 130
signification, 1, 161–2
similarity (see also: difference),
124, 157–9
Simmons, K. Merinda, 110–12
Skynyrd, Lynyrd, 88
slave-breaker, 101
slavery, 85 ff.
as coerced labor, 86
effects of, 85 ff.
history of, 85, 91–3
as not localized, 91
representations of, 86, 101
slaves as capital, 87
"a Southern problem," 85
Smart, Ninian, 17
Smith, Jonathan Z., 49
Smith, Leslie Dorrough, 71–2, 134,
138, 153–5
*Smokey and the Bandit*, 83

*Sneakers* (1992), 109
social groups
    as collaborative, 140–1, 151
    as constructed, 124, 141
    as fabricated, 124, 141
    formation, 124, 140
    as myth, 118, 124
    as not homogeneous, 118
    as performance, 140–1
    as situated, 141
socialism, 111
socio-economic systems, 83 ff., 91
    as class, 134
    as taken-for-granted, 87
Somers, Margaret, 93
South, the, 10, 82 ff.
space
    as contested, 78
    as religious, 78
    as secular, 78
Spielberg, Steven, 24
status, social, 23
Sterry, Eugene, 67–8
straw-man argument, 122
subjectivity, 29 ff., 34
    as collaboration, 3
    historicity of, 7
superstition, 47
Sutcliffe, Steve, 14
syncretism, 5

tarot, 19
tax system, 83
territory, 35–6
text
    interpretation of, 79
    as religious, 79
Thanksgiving (US), 78
theology, 17, 111

Thermopylae, Battle of, 30
thrift, 42 ff.
timelessness, 34
Torah study, 25
Touna, Vaia, viii, 6, 34–5, 95 ff., 99
    as Touna, 98, 99
    as Vaya, 95
tradition, 124
    food, 81
Twain, Mark, 52

UCL Bentham Project n.d., 103
UFO, 15
United Kingdom, 39
universalism, 26, 106
University of Alabama, 82, 85, 88, 93
    Foster Auditorium, 84
us/them, 89 ff., 152, 162
    as other, 134, 161
    the other as exotic, 108, 161

vegetarianism, 79
    as category, 77
    diversity of, 73 ff., 77
    history of, 73
    as identity, 73 ff.
    motivation for, 73–4, 77
Voegelin, Eric, 48–9
Vosper, Gretta, 70

Wagner, Alex, 159
Wallace, George, 84
war, 26
    Peloponnesian War, 30
    US War in Vietnam, 147
    War on Terror, 137
    World War I, 35
    World War II, 25–6, 80

Warne, Randi, 12
Weber, Max, 8, 48, 117
West Hill United Church (Toronto), 70
Wiccan, 47
Woodhead, Linda, 38

worldviews, 17

Yannaras, Christos, 95–7
Young, Neil, 88

Zeno of Elea, 122

www.ingramcontent.com/pod-product-compliance
Lightning Source LLC
Chambersburg PA
CBHW061738270326
41928CB00011B/2291